LIVING WILLS & HEALTH CARE PROXIES

Assuring That Your End-of-Life Decisions Are Respected

MARTIN M. SHENKMAN, CPA, MBA, JD

and PATTI S. KLEIN, MD

Law Made Easy Press, LLC
Teaneck, New Jersey

To our clients, patients, friends, and families, who have allowed us to share with them and their loved ones their end-of-life journeys—not only their pain, sorrow, and difficulties, but ever more importantly, their dignity, compassion, and insights.

ACKNOWLEDGMENTS

Thanks to Kim Kennedy of CNN for her referral of Martin Shenkman to CNN for a news segment with Soledad O'Brien that became the nucleus for this book.

Our thanks go to many people who participated in the preparation of this book on such short notice. Tremendous thanks and acknowledgment to Zvi Adler for his research, writing, rewriting, and proofreading efforts. Margaret Haase provided considerable proofreading and redrafting efforts.

Thanks to Mark Giammanco for the cover design and to Rebecca Boroson and Jamie Janoff for their encouragement and editorial support for an initial article that crystallized the concept of this book. Thanks to Maggie Galvin, Esq. of Holy Name Hospital, Teaneck, New Jersey, for her input; Sidney Kess, Laura Tierney, and the Commerce Clearing House staff for their help on the living will article; Ronnie Roha of *Kiplingers* magazine for her insight and article; and to Rosalie Gross and the editorial staff at the *New Jersey Lawyer* for their insight, openmindedness, editorial assistance, and encouragement in publishing articles on religion and the law, a topic most in the legal profession have ignored. Finally, to Nancy Marcus Land of Publications Development Company of Texas and all her production staff for a great job.

Most importantly, our thanks to the many patients and clients whose trauma, tragedies, and pain, as well as hope, dignity, and compassion, have taught us so much. While living wills and health care proxies are legal documents and the decisions they address are medical in nature, the real lessons are taught by those life experiences that so many special people have allowed us to share with them. For that we are forever indebted. This book includes many stories of patients and clients, but also of friends and family. Their names and some details have been omitted to preserve their privacy and dignity, but we hope these stories will give some meaning to their journeys and ease yours.

MARTIN M. SHENKMAN, ESQ.
PATTI S. KLEIN, MD

Teaneck, New Jersey
December 2003

CONTENTS

1 END-OF-LIFE DECISIONS

THE TRAGEDY OF TERRI SCHIAVO

In February 1990, Terri Schiavo suffered a cardiac arrest (heart attack), which temporarily cut off oxygen to her brain, causing severe brain damage. Terri lives in a persistent vegetative state. She has no higher order brain function (no cerebral cortical function). Her husband served as her guardian, having responsibility for personal care decisions. In 1993, her parents, Bob and Mary Schindler, sued to have Terri's husband, Michael, replaced as her guardian. The case was dismissed. In 1998, her husband petitioned the court to have Terri's feeding tube removed. Perhaps he felt she had suffered enough; perhaps he wanted closure to a tragic, painful, and sad chapter in his life. While many ugly allegations have been made about him, what is really in his heart can never be known (and it is not the public's business in any event). In early 2000, the court authorized the removal of the feeding tube. Legal wrangling and tremendous publicity ensued over the removal of the tube. The legal battles pitting parents against husband, the pain of all of the parties, and the public disclosure of intensely personal family matters have made this young woman's tragedy a nightmare for her and all those concerned about her.

The tragedy affecting Terri Schiavo and her family was the subject of tremendous media attention. Sadly, many similar tragedies are common although they don't receive media attention. Therefore, don't assume that you and your loved ones are

1

immune. Don't assume that the gut-wrenching decisions and resulting family conflict won't affect you and your loved ones. They may unless you act affirmatively to avoid it.

WHAT STEPS CAN YOU TAKE TO AVOID THESE PROBLEMS?

How can you protect yourself, your spouse, your loved ones, and your children? The media frenzy following the case has highlighted the importance of taking steps, such as the signing of a living will, to avoid a repeat of the Schiavo tragedy. Perhaps if the tragedy motivates millions of Americans to take the necessary steps, some good can be found in the aftermath of so much pain.

Unfortunately, the Schiavo media frenzy vastly oversimplified the steps you need to take to protect yourself and your loved ones. Simple is good when it works, but often more is required. This book walks you through the decision-making process and helps you make the decisions and take steps to achieve protection for yourself, your children, your elderly parents, other family members, and other loved ones.

WHY PROTECTING YOUR END-OF-LIFE DECISIONS IS SO IMPORTANT

Few decisions are more important to you than how health care decisions will be made for you if you are not able to make them for yourself. There is no decision more final or more profound than the possible termination of life support. Most of us have experienced, or one day will experience, the gut-wrenching pain of agonizing over whether to authorize an end-of-life medical procedure. Dealing with the issues now will lessen that pain for you and your loved ones. Illness and death are not easy or pleasant topics. They are painful. They are often messy. But the pain and difficulties can be lessened dramatically, and this book shows you how. But if you don't act to affirmatively specify your wishes, they may not be known, and won't be followed.

Case Study

Many people, whether for personal or perhaps religious reasons, wish to be buried. When this important personal decision is not documented in a living will (usually on the assumption that "they know"), this simple wish may be violated. More than once we've heard of someone who was cremated, and only afterward did his or her request for burial (not cremation) come to light. Sadly, an important end-of-life wish can never be corrected. A modicum of planning could have avoided this situation.

Ending life support is not the only decision that may have to be made for you. Health care decisions address far more than just the cessation of life support. They include, as we explain in considerable detail in later chapters, a wide range of situations that require resolution—hospice care, nursing home care, organ donations, funeral services, and burial. Many of these elections have nothing to do with decisions about death. For example, designating a person to make health care decisions (a health care agent) can empower that person to make decisions if you are temporarily unable to, but have significant hope of a full recovery.

THE MORAL DILEMMA— THE HARD QUESTIONS

Should Terri Schiavo's feeding tube be removed? Perhaps by the time you read this book, the legal battle will be over. Or perhaps fate itself may take the decision away from the courts, legislatures, and family alike. Regardless of the outcome, the situation raises fundamental moral issues—issues you must address and resolve for yourself.

A substantial majority of adults believe that a patient should have a right to make his or her own medical decisions, including refusing medical treatment if dying or in an irreversible coma. What does this really mean? How should *dying* be defined? In the broadest sense, once born, we are all dying. How close must you be to death to be considered "dying"? Six months? One year? Even that is not particularly informative because even a few weeks of time to tell loved ones goodbye are invaluable. Myriad other medical possibilities other than dying and irreversible coma still need to be addressed. Of those who believe in end-of-life decision making, most are fairly restrictive in what they believe is appropriate. Significantly, many adults (some estimates are between 15 percent and 25 percent) believe that even terminally ill patients should receive all forms of medical treatment. The moral controversy is considerable.

If you are in a vegetative state, does it remain a moral imperative to continue your life? If you answer in the negative, how severe must your vegetative state be to justify the discontinuance of life support? If you have some brain activity, is that sufficient to warrant maintaining your life support? How much brain activity is necessary to maintain life support? If you ascribe to this approach, at what level of analysis should the argument stop? Should a severely retarded person be maintained? Unfair question? But is it? How far can the questions go?

How should the spectrum of possibilities of brain activity (vegetative state) be defined? How should it be measured? With what degree of certainty should it be measured?

What if you are terminally ill, but have some chance of recovery? Would a 20 percent chance of recovery be sufficient? Perhaps for some; maybe not for you. While few would argue that a 50-50 chance should be ignored, what about a 10 percent probability? 5 percent? How far? The questions bring to mind the biblical story of Abraham bargaining with God over the plight of the inhabitants of Sodom and Gomorrah. How many righteous people should be found in the cities for the cities to be spared? 50? 45? 40? 30? 20? 10? (Genesis 18:23–32). What is a sufficient probability of recovery to justify taking heroic actions to save your life? And how much life must you have to warrant saving? What quality of life is minimally necessary to justify approving medical intervention? Is the *quality* of life irrelevant to the decision, and do you feel *any* life is worth saving?

This book asks many questions. You must ask questions, as well, to help identify and crystalize your feelings. Discussions of these issues will also help your loved ones understand your true feelings.

THE LEGAL DILEMMA

A number of landmark court cases over the years have addressed important issues concerning end-of-life decisions. While you certainly don't need to be a lawyer to sign a living will, a bit of background on some of these cases and their implications to your decision making is helpful. No effort has been made to ensure that each of the cases summarized is current. The goal is instead to alert you to the issues and concerns you must address. Because the status of this entire area of the law is in flux and it is likely in the wake of the Terri Schiavo case that further legislation will be enacted, you should consult an elder law or estate planning expert for the appropriate legal documents to protect yourself. Remember also that the laws differ in significant ways from state to state, so you need to consult an expert in your state (see pp. 49–50, 124–125).

Schloendorff v. Society of New York Hospitals
102 N.E. 92 (NY 1914)

This early case included an oft-quoted statement of Judge Cardoza: "Every human being of adult years and sound mind has a right to determine what shall be done with his own body; and a surgeon who performs an operation without his patient's consent commits an assault for which he is liable in damages." This case was one of the initial and landmark decisions in affirming a patient's right to approve his or her own medical treatment.

In Re Quinlan 70 N.J. 10 (1976)

The issue in this case was whether the parents of a daughter, who was in a persistent vegetative state, could make a decision on their daughter's behalf to withdraw her from a respirator. Perhaps the court believed that the daughter was near death, regardless of continued life support. The court addressed the constitutional right every person has to self-determination and the common law (developed from court cases) right for everyone to give *informed consent* to a medical treatment. The court ultimately held that the parents could make the decision to withdraw the respirator. The parents effectively were given the approval to make a "substitute judgment" for the patient, who could not make a judgment. This case is a reminder of the difficulty of making decisions for someone who is not competent, especially for a child who has taken no action. Perhaps the best you can do is to prepare an emergency child medical form (Chapter 9) and encourage your child to take the steps outlined in this book when he or she attains the age of majority (status as a legal adult) in your state.

Superintendent of Belchertown State School v. Saikewicz 370 N.E.2d 417, 424–425 (Mass. 1977)

A key restriction on your right to determine your own medical care or lack of care, as the case may be, is the interests or responsibility your state's government has toward protecting individual patients. Each state views itself as having a responsibility to protect those who cannot protect themselves. State rights include four key matters:

1. Prevention of suicide.
2. Preservation of life: Each state has an interest in preserving the life of its citizens. However, that right should not necessarily override the right of a competent patient to make a decision as to directing the course of his or her own life. Your state will have the strongest interest in protecting your life if you are incompetent or somehow vulnerable to abuse (e.g., you're under the age of adult status).
3. Protecting the interests of innocent parties: If, for example, you are young and have minor children, the state

might be concerned about the support, welfare, and emotional effect on your children if you are taken off life support. If a medical procedure would have to be performed on you to save your unborn child, but the procedure would violate your religious beliefs (e.g., a blood transfusion), the state may act to protect you.

4. Maintaining the ethical integrity of the medical profession: Your personal wishes cannot be used to compel a physician to violate the physician's code of professional conduct. Every physician takes the Hippocratic Oath to preserve life. Your personal wishes should not compel a physician to violate his or her oath.

It is clear that each state has interests or concerns in this process as well. This issue was loudly emphasized by the Florida legislature's ruling that Terri Schiavo's feeding tube had to be reinserted. Why would a state be concerned about what should be purely individual personal matters? Because the conclusion that it is a personal, not a state, matter is not clear. A simple example illustrates why a state government must act to protect those who cannot protect themselves.

Example: A severely retarded man is ill with terminal cancer. Independent of his illness, he is unable to comprehend or make medical decisions. It would have been impossible for him to sign a living will or health care proxy because of his mental retardation. The hospital in which he is being treated determines that his prognosis is perhaps a month to live, and that month is assuredly going to be a month of severe pain. He is presently being kept alive by a ventilator and feeding tube. The hospital determines that, from a humane standpoint, the ventilator should be discontinued. Should they be able to discontinue the ventilator?

An additional fact comes to light. The severely retarded patient's financial resources are substantial as a result of money his deceased parents left in a trust fund. The cousins who have been encouraging the medical staff to remove the ventilator stand to inherit millions. There is clearly a need for state law to protect such a helpless patient to be sure it is really in his best interest, not that of his greedy cousins, to remove the ventilator.

The problem with this case is that the patient was never able to communicate his wishes because he never had the capacity to make them known. Should the hospital, or all of us collectively as a society, have the right to make a decision for him? The additional facts in the example would probably offend almost anyone. With this backdrop, how different is it when an intelligent person does not make his or her health care wishes known, and then, because of illness, is unable to make or communicate health care wishes? Is he or she really in any different position than the severely retarded man in the preceding examples? If the state government does not step in, typically through the enactment of laws, to protect helpless patients such as the severely retarded man or even the patient who can no longer make a decision, what is to prevent any health care provider, or perhaps a niece waiting to inherit, from requesting that medical efforts be ceased or life support withdrawn? The government has a vested interest in protecting those who cannot protect themselves.

The lesson to be learned from this case is important. If you would ever wish life support to be withheld or withdrawn, you must clearly communicate that wish so that the state will not feel compelled to protect your interests.

In Re Quackenbush 156 N.J. Super. 252 (Ch. Div. 1978)

A competent adult, able to make decisions, did not wish to authorize a procedure to amputate his leg, a procedure necessary to save his life. The court affirmed the competent adult's right to make a decision. This is a key concept in protecting your end-of-life wishes. You need to make decisions while you are clearly competent to do so.

If a patient is unable to make decisions and has not left clear and convincing evidence of what health care decisions are desired, the decisions may have to be made by a court-appointed surrogate. With no guidance, the surrogate will have to make decisions based on what is in the best interests of the patient. What might this mean?

Barber v. Superior Court 195 Cal. Rptr. 484 (Cal. App. 1983)

This court decision provided some guidance. "Under this standard, such factors as the relief of suffering, the preservation or restoration of functioning and the quality as well as the extent of life sustained may be considered. Finally, since most people are concerned about the well-being of their loved ones, the surrogate may take into account the impact of the decisions on those people closest to the patient." Although this quote is informative and does provide some guidance, it is vague. The vagueness of this standard and the uncertainty as to how various family members or others might interpret it should motivate you to document your wishes. This quote also points out an important point that most living wills and health care proxies ignore: How will your decisions affect your loved ones? This issue should be addressed with some care and is discussed in Chapter 3 in the context of funeral arrangements that provide the most solace to your survivors, the continuation of life support when the impact is prolongation of suffering of loved ones, and in other contexts.

In Re Conroy 98 N.J. 321 (1985)

Many of the court cases address situations of patients who are in a persistent vegetative state, and there is certainty that they will never be able to make and communicate decisions concerning health care. This case involved a somewhat different situation and, as such, provides further insight into how courts might analyze an end-of-life decision. The patient was an elderly nursing home resident who could not make a decision for herself. She was not, however, in a persistent vegetative state, and she was not deemed medically to be permanently unconscious. The court, therefore, decided that it was not appropriate to use the analysis of the *In Re Quinlan* case of letting someone make a "substituted decision." The court instead provided for a three-part test:

1. *The Limited Objective Test:* Medical treatments can be withheld or discontinued if there is some "trustworthy" evidence that the patient would have refused the treatment involved and in the particular circumstances the pain or other burdens of the patient's condition outweigh the benefits to the patient of prolonged life. By contrast, in the most recent case concerning Terri Schiavo, it seems that she was in no pain. Her husband explained on the "Larry King Show" on national television that the evidence that she would not want to continue on life support was a brief comment she made in response to a television show. Should this have sufficed?

2. *The Pure Objective Test:* If there is no evidence at all as to the patient's wishes, life-sustaining treatment may be withheld only if the pain to the patient is so severe that prolonging the patient's life would be considered inhumane.

3. *The Subjective Test:* If there is clear and convincing evidence of the patient's subjective intent, that intent should be honored.

The best method of communicating this intent is to have a detailed living will and health care proxy. With so much uncertainty in making end-of-life decisions, appointing an agent to make decisions at that time, based on knowledge of your condition and in consultation with medical experts, is a reasonable approach. However, given how subjective, uncertain, and personal the decisions can be, a living will outlining many of your feelings and certainly your express beliefs can help address the issues identified in this and other cases.

This case addressed another controversial issue. The court decided to equate the withholding of nutrition and hydration to the withholding of a respirator or other life-sustaining treatments. Many people, particularly those with fundamental religious beliefs, may find that the withholding of nutrition and hydration is particularly problematic, even akin to starving someone to death. This is why our discussions and sample forms encourage you to specifically address how you feel about this specific issue.

In Re Farrell 108 N.J. 335 (1987)

This case involved a woman dying from amyotrophic lateral sclerosis, or Lou Gehrig's disease. She clearly indicated that she wanted to be removed from life support, specifically a respirator. The court weighed the interests that the state might have in the matter against her right to decline life support and upheld the patient's right to determine her treatment. The court, however, required two independent physicians to determine that the patient was competent to make the decisions and that she was fully informed. One lesson of this case is clear: Make your decisions early, while you are able to and while you are demonstrably competent.

In Re Peter 108 N.J. 365 (1987)

While this case addressed a number of issues, some particular to New Jersey law, one conclusion has a general and important lesson. Because the patient had not made a specific designation of a surrogate decision maker and there was no clear and convincing evidence (proof) of the patient's subjective intent, a guardian had to be appointed by the court. (The concept of guardianship is discussed in Chapter 7.) Avoid the costs, difficulties, and delays that guardianship can create by signing a living will, health care proxy, and related documents. Completing a revocable living trust (see Chapter 10) will also help you avoid these difficulties by filling in some of the gaps and related matters that the living will and health care proxy may not always address.

Gray by Gray v. Romeo 697 F. Supp. 580, 585 (D.R.I. 1988)

The federal district court for Rhode Island held in a significant case that each person has a right to privacy, and that right has fundamental implications to the provision of and refusal to accept medical care. A key passage from this case provides important insight:

> . . . the Court's decisions have repeatedly affirmed the principle of individual self-determination. A person has the right, subject to important state interests, to control fundamental medical decisions that affect his or her own body. This right, whether described as the principle of personal autonomy, the right of self-determination, or the right of privacy, is properly grounded in the liberties protected by the Fourteenth Amendment's [of the United States Constitution] due process clause. This right is also grounded in the notion of an individual's dignity and interest in bodily integrity.

Courts recognize certain rights you have to control the medical care you do, or don't, receive. But you must communicate those wishes. In crafting the language for your living will, you should emphasize what it means to you to protect your individual dignity and your bodily integrity.

Cruzan v. Missouri Department of Health 497 U.S. 261 (1990)

This was a U.S. Supreme Court decision: "It cannot be disputed that the Due Process Clause (of the Fourteenth Amendment to the United States Constitution) protects an interest in life as well as an interest in refusing life-sustaining medical treatment." The court also said: "The principle that a competent person has a constitutionally protected liberty interest in refusing unwanted medical treatment may be inferred from our prior decisions." The question in this case was whether there was enough evidence of the now incompetent patient's wishes concerning medical treatment to carry out those wishes. Implicit throughout the majority opinion and expressly stated in Justice O'Connor's concurrence and all the dissents (except Justice Scalia's) was acceptance of the proposition that an advance written directive would have easily satisfied the clear and convincing evidence standard imposed by the Missouri Supreme Court.

Washington v. Harper **494 U.S. 210 (1990)**

The U.S. Supreme Court decided that prison inmates suffering from mental disorders possess "a significant liberty interest in avoiding the unwanted administration of antipsychotic drugs under the Due Process Clause of the Fourteenth Amendment." The court also observed that "[t]he forcible injection of medication into a nonconsenting person's body represents a substantial interference with that person's liberty."

There is no indication in this case that you must be in a terminal, irreversible, incurable, or untreatable condition, or in a permanently unconscious or vegetative state to enjoy your fundamental Fourteenth Amendment right to refuse treatment and otherwise control what is done to your body. Indeed, the Cruzan court did not question whether incompetents had fundamental rights under the federal Constitution. Therefore, if you have prepared your living will while competent and later become incompetent, your wishes as expressed in the living will (and health care proxy) should be respected as if you were then competent.

Planned Parenthood of Southeastern Pennsylvania v. Casey **112 S. Ct. 2791, 2811 (1992)**

This case was resolved in 1992. The U.S. Supreme Court confirmed: "viability marks the earliest point at which the state's interest in fetal life is constitutionally adequate to justify a legislative ban on therapeutic abortions." As a result, you should have the right to abort your pregnancy before viability. In addition, even if your fetus is viable, the U.S. Supreme Court has said that mothers need not be exposed to increased medical risks for the sake of their fetuses and that the state's interest in the potential life of the fetus is insufficient to override the mother's interest in preserving her own health.

In Re Doe 632 N.E.2d 326 (Ill. App. Ct.), cert. denied, 114 S. Ct. 1198 (1994)

In this case, it was held that the refusal of treatment by women with viable fetuses should be respected. On this basis, it is you who should decide what is to be done to yourself and your fetus.

In Re Fiori (Penn. Sup. Ct. Apr. 1996)

A patient was unable to make medical decisions, and there was no sufficient evidence of the decisions the patient would have wanted made. The court recognized that in this situation close family members could make the decision with two qualified physicians to withdraw life support of the patient who was in a persistent vegetative state. Given the tremendous diversity in religious, moral, and ethical views even within the same family, this result may not be what you wish to occur.

In Re Fetus Brown (Ill. App. Ct. Dec. 1997)

A competent pregnant women was a Jehovah's Witness and refused blood transfusions following surgery, which may have saved both her life and the life of her viable fetus. The state believed it had a right to protect the unborn fetus, but did that right outweigh the pregnant woman's right to refuse medical treatment? The appellate court held that the state could not override the decisions of a competent pregnant woman. The woman had a constitutional right and common law (state case law) right to refuse treatment.

Knight et al. v. Beverly Health Care Bay Manor Health Care Center (Ala. Sup. Ct. Aug. 2001)

This case points out one of the significant fallacies of living wills. Many people assume that merely signing a living will or health care proxy ensures that whatever decisions they've made will be carried out. It is not so simple. In this case, the patient was diagnosed as being in a persistent vegetative state, and some family members wanted to withdraw the feeding tube. Other family members disagreed with the court's conclusion that the patient was in a persistent vegetative state. The appellate court (the higher court that reviewed the initial or lower court's decision) determined (held) that there must be clear and convincing proof that the patient was vegetative for the living will to become effective.

Sampson et al. v. State of Alaska **No. 5474 (Alaska Sup. Ct. Sept. 21, 2001)**

Competent adults who were terminally ill were denied the right of physician-assisted suicide. The court held that physician-assisted suicide was not within their constitutional right to liberty or privacy. This result is typical and provides a limit on how far you can proceed in achieving personal end-of-life wishes.

Conclusion

In spite of much of the recent controversy in the media about living wills and end-of-life decisions, based on federal and state constitutional law and stated common law, you should have the personal right to demand that the instructions set forth in your living will be followed regardless of your medical condition.

YOU NEED MORE THAN A LIVING WILL

Protecting yourself and your loved ones takes more than signing a simple one-page form. You, your wishes, and your family circumstances are never as simple as a one-page boilerplate (standard language) form. Such a form is unlikely to address many critical legal and practical issues. A generic Internet web site is unlikely to address the myriad personal and religious issues that can ruin a family and desecrate solemn end-of-life rituals. No family is one-dimensional.

Here are the steps you need to take:

Step 1: *Read this book and think through carefully, and practically, each of the documents and steps involved.* Highlight passages that are important to you. Make notes in the margin. Write "NO!" by points you disagree with. Circle issues you want to address. Dog-ear pages. Let this be a working manual that also serves as a guide to your family. If you are certain about the answer to any of the questions raised in this book, make a notation of your answer. Doing so will make this book more useful to you, and it can become a resource of tremendous importance to your loved ones in trying to understand your feelings and beliefs in the future. When you later consult with a physician to discuss the implications of your decisions, perhaps with a social worker or religious adviser, and finally a lawyer, your annotations and comments on this book can be used as a guideline to refining your decisions and eventually incorporating them into formal documents expressing your wishes.

Step 2: *Sign a living will.* A living will is a legal document in which you specify personal health care decisions, end-of-life decisions, funeral and burial preferences, and other important personal items. (See Chapter 2.)

Step 3: *Sign a health care proxy or a health care power of attorney.* In these legal documents, you designate a person (agent) to make health care decisions. (See Chapter 5.)

Step 4: *If you have minor children, sign an emergency child medical form.* This form is a legal document in which you authorize a designated person to make medical decisions for a minor (under legal age) child in your absence (you're on vacation and leave your young son with Aunt Nellie or a nanny) and provide important medical information to help health care providers. (See Chapter 9.)

Step 5:   Make Steps 1 through 4 part of an overall plan. To really provide the protection you and your loved ones need, these documents should be completed as part of a comprehensive estate and financial plan. It doesn't have to be expensive or a difficult process, but signing a health care proxy and living will alone will never provide all the protection you need. Consider a revocable living trust, will, review of health and long-term care insurance, life insurance, disability insurance, and other practical steps (discussed in Chapter 10). But for any of these documents to work, you have to invest the emotional capital to understand and work through the tough decisions involved.

UNDERSTANDING A DO NOT RESUSCITATE (DNR) ORDER

To make the right decisions, you need to understand what a "Do Not Resuscitate" (DNR) order means. This discussion is not a value judgment on whether you should or should not permit a DNR, but rather an appeal to you to try to understand the consequences of the decisions you make as an agent for someone else and in preparing your own living will. You should read the following and reflect on what it means in the graphic physical sense to "code" an 85-year-old grandparent with multiple chronic medical problems.

Case Study

Picture this unfortunate scene repeated thousands of times a day. The nurse goes into grandpa's room for routine blood pressure monitoring. She notices that grandpa is unresponsive. The nurse calls the operator to "Call a code in Room 122." The resuscitation team consisting of physicians, nurses, and respiratory therapists (approximately 10 people) crowd around grandpa's bedside. CPR is administered. Advanced cardiac life support (ACLS) measures are started. If grandpa doesn't have an intravenous line, one is inserted so medications, such as adrenaline, can be given. Sometimes the only intravenous access is via a large vein, either in the groin, the neck, or the upper chest. A breathing tube is inserted through his windpipe so artificial respiration can ensue. Monitors are attached. It's invasive. It is messy. It is traumatic. You'd like not to think about it during those trying moments, but the two-page boilerplate form that grandpa signed doesn't seem to address the complex medical issues that have arisen.

Is this really what you want to put your grandfather through? How many times should you put him through this trauma? Do you really understand the impact on him? If grandpa has already had several strokes and is in a vegetative state, is this how you would want his life prolonged? Most family members who refuse to issue a DNR are never there to see the potential horrors of what resuscitation can mean. Too many people want to avoid the guilt that they didn't do enough to save grandpa. But the decision should not be based on your guilt.

The opposite perspective must also be considered. Many people will undoubtedly sign standard living wills and too readily authorize a DNR. Have you ever spoken to a physician or religious pastor who has been at the bedside of someone for whom the family has given up hope but then recovers? Will the pendulum now swing to the opposite direction in the wake of the Schiavo media frenzy with families too easily authorizing a DNR without adequate forethought?

These two extremes highlight the decision process of what must be addressed in your living will. An actual case study illustrates.

Case Study

A well-known New York City physician, Dr. F., tells a patient story that is not uncommon. A person (not then his patient) went to the emergency room where he was diagnosed with an aggressive cancer and was advised that little could be done other than palliative care. Dr. F. was consulted and scheduled the patient for surgery. The patient lived for another six years—a result that Dr. F. called "a gift." "Everyone involved in the case had given up hope, yet the patient was given six more years to enjoy life and live with his family. He worked for nearly four more years; he returned to visit family in Greece several times." Had someone taken the stance of palliative care rather than aggressive intervention, all this would have been lost. While this was a clear victory for pursuing life, there is more to the story. Six years later when the patient was near death, the patient's wife, as his agent under a living will and health care proxy, authorized morphine to relieve her husband's severe pain, and shortly thereafter he passed away. The widow was distraught and believed that had she not authorized the use of morphine, her husband wouldn't have died. In spite of six years of life, which even the world-renowned physician deemed "a gift," the widow was distraught and blamed herself for his death.

This case study illustrates several important points to consider with respect to end-of-life planning. While this case result was perhaps in part due to the capabilities of a world-renowned physician, miraculous recoveries do occur. Other competent physicians who examined the same patient had reached a different conclusion. These events are not really susceptible to statistical study. So how do you factor this possibility into the planning, discussions, drafting of documents, and carrying out of your wishes? The second important point illustrated is the pain and trauma this process almost always visits on those vested with decision-making authority—here, a wife who was fortunate enough to enjoy most of six years with her mate. This is the same wife who for some period of time after the initial diagnosis would have made a Faustian bargain for six weeks. Yet she felt tremendous guilt. The attending physician assured her that her husband's demise was due to the illness, not her decision to relieve pain. He tried to compassionately help her focus on the wonderful bonus years they might never have had. But her guilt continued. If this widow could experience such guilt over merely authorizing pain relief in these circumstances, can you imagine the emotional upheaval your agent could feel in authorizing a failed medical procedure or the cessation of life support? Your tackling the tough issues in this book and discussing them in advance with your loved ones can minimize and, in many situations, avoid entirely the pain, guilt, and emotional upheaval of those having to make decisions for you. If you love them, you owe them this much.

DON'T WAIT FOR A TRAGEDY TO STRIKE

The time to make your most important life and death decisions and the many other health and related decisions discussed in this book is not when you are admitted to the hospital for emergency surgery. Hospital personnel will likely ask if you have a living will or health care proxy. If you do not, they may provide you with a form to sign. How are you supposed to objectively reflect on what you want in such circumstances? Who will be available to discuss the issues? Who can you consult with about the implications of the decisions? Ensuring that your end-of-life decisions are respected requires advance planning.

Few people have a problem discussing the purchase of life insurance, but most people have considerable difficulty addressing health care decisions. Studies have estimated that only about 20 percent of Americans have a living will or health care proxy. While this is a huge improvement from the mere 8 percent estimated to have had advance directives in 1989, it is still woefully inadequate. Life insurance pays only in the event of death. Living wills and health care proxies often apply to situations that do not result in death. Although none of these are pleasant thoughts, perhaps they provide a different perspective to encourage you to address your health care issues. If you can talk about *life* insurance, you should be able to talk about *living wills.*

Case Study

A close friend of mine, not only an attorney, but an attorney who worked in the surrogates court (the court where wills are processed and estates handled), phoned me one afternoon. After the typical old buddy "How 'ya beens," he informed me of his battle with pancreatic cancer and the prognosis for what was left of his life. When we both finished crying, he explained to me that he had no documents, no planning, nothing. We worked at his hospital bedside to get his affairs and documents in order. On more than one occasion when the nurse came with his scheduled pain medication, he refused so that he would be lucid enough to address the issues important to him. His struggles during his last weeks demonstrated a dignity that was truly inspiring and a love and concern for not only the family he was leaving behind, but also the charities and many close friends. These struggles could have been addressed with far greater ease and far less physical pain before illness struck. But like so many, he couldn't have imagined that such a tragedy would befall him—a healthy and young individual. If a bright, knowledgeable attorney, who worked in the very specialty dealing with living wills, had not addressed these issues, don't assume anyone has.

My friend, with all his knowledge and expertise, sadly waited for tragedy to strike. Don't. The biblical figure Moses knew in advance that he would not enter the Promised Land. He knew his life was drawing to an end. He used that time to address and bless his followers, transition leadership, and put his affairs in order (Deuteronomy 33:1). Few of us will ever be blessed with an advance tap on the shoulder informing us that the end is near. We all have to prepare for the inevitable before the inevitable arrives.

TALKING TO YOUR LOVED ONES ABOUT YOUR HEALTH CARE WISHES

This point, although noted previously, is so vital that it warrants repeating. The best legal documents won't ensure that all your wishes are carried out. The decisions that will be made require thought and sensitivity because no legal document can possibly embody the myriad emotions, medical considerations, health conditions, and other factors. Communicating to your loved ones and, in particular, those people you designate to make decisions for you (agents) is essential. No, these discussions won't be easy, but they are vital.

TALKING TO YOUR LOVED ONES ABOUT THEIR HEALTH CARE WISHES

Health care issues may affect any of your loved ones. If your parents (or other elderly or infirm family members) are living, have they signed the appropriate documents? If not, how will you be able to help them? Taking all the steps in this book to protect your end-of-life wishes does nothing to minimize the pain you will have in dealing with end-of-life decisions for your loved ones.

Caution: Don't ever presume that any family member, loved one, or friend has taken the proper precautions if he or she hasn't spoken to you about it in detail and let you see signed legal documents (or copies so you know it's been done). Most people simply haven't addressed these issues. The vast majority (perhaps as high as 70 percent) of lawyers in our country don't even have wills. If most lawyers haven't addressed their own wills, how likely is it that your aunt has addressed a living will, which involves much more difficult and personal decisions than a will?

The first step is to open a dialogue with your parent (aunt, uncle, or other loved one). Success in addressing these sensitive personal matters will depend on cooperation from that person. Without a dialogue and then cooperation, there will be little you can do to help. Often, an immediate open discussion is not practical. You may have to focus on the alternative or indirect approaches. Choose a time and situation that is most comfortable and best suited for your loved one and his or her circumstances. Perhaps you could begin by discussing issues that will give him or her comfort in later years, before delving into the difficult end-of-life issues. Depending on your loved one's temperament, you might begin with a discussion of his or her financial security, your own estate planning, charitable giving, or religious issues. Something less difficult and final than living will issues is often an easier icebreaker. Many elderly worry that their life savings will be dissipated in nursing home fees or estate taxes. Identifying an external issue such as taxes is often an easy starting point. No one wants to pay extra taxes. Select and tailor the approach that you believe may work, go easy, move slowly, and be sensitive.

Older members of the family are often loath to discuss personal estate planning issues, such as living wills and health care proxies, with the younger generations. They were raised in a time when discussing money was considered crass, and certainly discussing their personal situation with their children was viewed as inappropriate. Thus, when should you begin the dialogue? What do you say? How do you say it?

First, when to begin it should be governed by the old adage: One step at a time. Don't address everything at once. The earlier you begin this process with your parents, the less they will feel you're a vulture circling, waiting for the day you can get your hands on their money. Try not to wait until old age and infirmity have set in. Rather, begin discussions with your parents when the specter of death is not looming. Find times when your parents are at their leisure, relaxed, and unthreatened. Ask your parents if they have a living will and health care proxy to address medical issues. Ask if they understand that medical decisions will be made for them, or perhaps they will be kept on life support long after they might wish to be. If your parents have strong religious convictions, without a living will to make them known, those criteria may be completely ignored in their treatment.

If your parents are not comfortable even broaching the topic with you, it is often helpful to open the dialogue by discussing the steps you have taken in planning for your own living will (or if that is too sensitive, your own estate plan). This approach achieves the dual purpose of ensuring you do not ignore planning for your own future, as well as opening the dialogue with your parents in a nonthreatening manner. For example, if you want to address the topic of writing a living will, begin by outlining the directives you have placed in your own. If you've named a parent as an agent in your document or want your parents' input as to religious or other personal decisions, seek their counsel. This provides a positive and deferential way to open the discussion—you are seeking their advice. And don't discount what the knowledge of age and having lost friends and family have taught them. In their answers, you may also find the answer to your question of how to get your parents to discuss their own planning. Ask whether they agree with the decisions you have made and whether your decisions are in any way similar to the decisions they made when drawing up their living wills.

Personal Comment: With all this great advice, I must have been a natural at talking with my parents about this subject. Truth be told, I put off my father's overtures to address this matter for so long that at one point he called and informed me that if I didn't help with their planning, he was going to hire the most overpriced estate planner he could find to do the job. So I knuckled under and helped them. It's a difficult topic to address, even for someone who deals with it everyday.

Once an exchange is begun about estate planning, it usually becomes much simpler to then direct the conversation toward a discussion of the other person's living will and other related decisions. This kind of discussion often cannot take place at one time or in merely a few hours. There are many issues to be addressed and many decisions to be made. Every decision will require forethought, planning, and sufficient attention to ensure that important details have not been forgotten. What constitutes sufficient time will vary by age, gender, religion, size of the estate, health requirements, and other individual needs.

The knowledge that they will die in accordance with the religious values with which they lived their lives may bring great comfort to your parents in their waning years. Without communication, you cannot possibly know what your parents or other loved one may wish. The extent of wishes that might be important to them is broad but, without their clarification, difficult or impossible to know. Many people want to die in the comfort of their own home unhampered by myriad medical paraphernalia, tubes, hoses, equipment, and the heroic and often painful and taxing procedures that accompany them. The knowledge that they will have the peacefulness of dying at home among family and friends may bring some people comfort. Others want every heroic effort modern science can provide to prolong their life. Some wish to go further and, through cryogenics, ensure that medical efforts only future knowledge may provide might be available as well.

Case Study

One client, a university professor of some renown, specified in his living will that he be cremated and that a letter be sent to his students and former students inviting them to a ceremony on the top of a local mountain, where his ashes would be thrown to the wind while a poem he wrote was to be recited.

However you may feel about the requests, they were his last wishes and certainly should be respected. While your or your parents' last wishes may be far more pedestrian, without asking questions, no one can really know.

The knowledge that you cared enough to ensure that their last days will be spent in accordance with whatever their unique wishes might be will bring you and your parents even closer together. Be sensitive to the needs of your parents on a spiritual as well as physical level. The care you take now in ensuring that both these needs are met will go far in reassuring your parents of your good intentions. The more kindly they view your offer of assistance, the easier it will be for you to involve yourself in planning and the less likely there will be disputes, family arguments, or legal entanglements later.

INVOLVING THE RIGHT PEOPLE TO HELP

Addressing end-of-life decisions is a process that, when done well, requires more than merely the help of an attorney. The process ideally should involve input from several different types of people.

Family and Loved Ones

As stressed throughout this book, you need to involve your family and loved ones in the decision process, or at minimum inform them of what you've decided and their role in the process (if any). Whom you involve and whom you inform is a very personal decision, and there are no guidelines. A spouse or partner obviously has to be informed. Parents probably should be informed as well. If you have adult children, depending on their temperament, age, and role, perhaps they should be informed. If your children are still young (which depends on their maturity, not the legal age of majority or their biological age), perhaps they needn't be informed. While most people name immediate family members to be their decision makers (agents) in these documents, this is not always the case. Anyone you name as agent must first be asked if he or she is willing to serve (don't push), and if agreeable must be informed of your decisions, preferably in detail.

Medical Care Adviser

Living wills and health care proxies are legal documents prepared by lawyers. But the issues they address are in large part medical issues. Few lawyers really have the requisite understanding of what a DNR order, or gastrostomy tube is, to advise you on many vital issues. You need to discuss the decision-making process with someone with medical knowledge. While this might be your physician, it might be anyone else with whom you have a relationship or who is willing to spend the time. If you are being treated for a severe medical condition, you should discuss your general decisions with your attending physician (and probably provide him or her with a copy or original of your documents when they are completed). Your living will should address issues pertaining to every known medical condition.

Social Worker, Psychologist, or Other Mental Health Professional

If you are facing a terminal illness or severe health condition, you and your loved ones will benefit from discussing matters with a social worker or other mental health professional. If you have doubts or considerable discomfort about discussing these issues with particular family members, professional guidance and even participation can be a big plus. What approaches will give you the most comfort? What decisions might give your loved ones the most solace and least pain? If you are not involving a religious adviser in the process, consider a consultation with a mental health professional. The outside, objective advice might prove invaluable.

Religious Adviser

If appropriate (and even if not meaningful to you personally but important to your loved ones), a religious adviser should be involved in the process. Studies have shown that more than 90 percent of Americans believe in God or a higher being of some form. Ignoring religious sentiments, therefore, in crafting your end-of-life decisions may be a tremendous oversight. Chapter 4 provides insight into the issues raised by a number of religious beliefs. Whatever your religious affiliation, the decisions are so important and the knowledge is so specialized and unique to each religious perspective that the best way to address religion is to review your end-of-life decisions. Whenever feasible, discuss your actual living will and health care proxy with your religious adviser to be certain that your wishes are met.

Attorney

The bottom line is that you need a health care proxy and living will, perhaps more. These are legal documents that should be completed by an attorney. Although there are many free forms and documents you can obtain and this book has many, you should not, as a nonlawyer, complete your own documents any more than as a patient you should perform your own surgery (hold the mirror a bit higher so I can see where to make the incision). You can dramatically improve your results, ensure that your personal wishes are reflected, and save substantial costs if you handle the process correctly. To do this, do your homework. There are no quick fixes. Paying a lawyer a lot of money so you can avoid the tough decisions or the time it takes to complete the steps outlined in this book will ensure you an expensive legal document, nothing more. If you think through the issues involved and discuss them as advised in this book, you will minimize the clock ticks that your attorney charges you for.

Seek professional help; get a specialist. To have the issues addressed properly, you want an attorney who devotes a substantial part of his or her practice to nothing but estate planning. Start with recommendations from your accountant, insurance agent, or financial planner. They deal with estate planning experts all the time. Next, look up the attorney in the *Martindale-Hubbell* law directory available online. If you prefer paper, most local libraries should have a copy of the actual text. It lists a rating for the attorney and the firm where the attorney works. It also gives background information on the attorney. Next, call the attorney to confirm that his or her focus is estate planning or elder law. Discuss fees upfront. Most specialists bill on an hourly basis. How can an attorney quote you a fixed fee for a living will and health care proxy given the myriad decisions and issues involved? If you need a fixed fee, what happens if you want to address issues in your documents that require more thought or time? What happens to the fixed fee if the meeting proceeds quickly because you've thought through all the key issues in advance? To get some comfort, you can ask for a budget, but do you really want a fixed price?

A TOUGH MEETING OF EVERYONE INVOLVED

If you, or a loved one, are already facing a terminal illness, consider having a meeting with key family members, a social worker or psychologist, your religious adviser, if any, and your lawyer to not only discuss and resolve issues in your documents, but also help everyone deal with the imminent death. Perhaps viewed as advance bereavement counseling, this approach can mollify the otherwise inevitable difficulties. Whether this meeting has to take place in your hospital room, at a hospice facility, or your home, the clarity and comfort it can provide can be significant. Having experienced advisers present for the discussion will enable you to develop a better understanding of all the options available to you, from hospice, palliative care, to medical intervention. The help of the various advisers will enable you to communicate your feelings. Planning your remaining time in such an informative and supportive environment will assure you the maximum benefit (as you define the term) during your last days. Having persons to be charged with implementing the decisions in the room and the benefit of an experienced social worker or psychologist at hand will make their task less traumatic. This will be a very difficult, but worthwhile, meeting.

QUESTIONS TO CONSIDER

1. Have you thought about end-of-life decisions?
2. If you are young and healthy, perhaps you can handle the process in a more generic manner by simply appointing a parent, spouse, and other responsible loved one to serve as your agent under a health care proxy and defer the more detailed decisions embodied in a living will until a later age. Would this approach encourage your proceeding?
3. Do you have a living will? A health care proxy? Do your parents or other elderly loved ones have them?
4. Have you spoken with your loved ones about possible medical care scenarios for them and yourself?
5. Who might you speak with about these issues if you are uncomfortable addressing them with family?

CHAPTER SUMMARY

The unfortunate tragedy of Terri Schiavo underscores the importance of making end-of-life decisions before a medical emergency arises. These decisions, if incorporated into properly prepared legal documents, will help you as well as other family members deal more effectively with difficult issues that are likely to occur in the future. It's not sufficient to fill out a standard form living will and assume all is taken care of. It is unlikely to be. There are a number of steps you must take, all of which have been outlined in this chapter, and which are explored in greater depth in the following chapters. Steps include talking to loved ones, involving or hiring the right people to advise you, and signing a health care proxy and living will, which address completely the end-of-life decisions that you are contemplating.

2 GENERAL ISSUES AFFECTING YOUR LIVING WILL

INTRODUCTION TO LIVING WILLS

Your living will is a broad statement of any significant personal health and related care issues that are important to you, your loved ones, and your circumstances. A living will is one of the most important and personal documents you will ever sign. It is also one of the most controversial, misunderstood, and misapplied legal documents. As with too many important decisions, living wills have become a "quick fix." Sign a quick one-page standard form with your lawyer and your worries are over. Unfortunately, important legal, financial, religious, and medical issues cannot be addressed in such a superficial manner. Guidance is needed to help you through the process of properly communicating your wishes.

The following discussion reviews many of the general issues that you should understand in beginning the process of formulating the contents of your living will. Chapter 3 discusses more specific personalizing issues for you to address, and Chapter 4 completes the living will discussion with an analysis of religious issues.

USING THIS CHAPTER AND THE TEAR-OUT LIVING WILL FORM

This chapter explains what a living will is and advises you how to make decisions and obtain the best protection and comfort from this document. This discussion provides you with a method of communicating your wishes and identifying questions or concerns you may have. You can then complete the tear-out form in Chapter 13 and retain an attorney to formalize the document to ensure that it meets the laws of your state. With the detail of the tear-out form at hand, your lawyer can more thoroughly and economically assist you in the preparation of a comprehensive living will. Starting with a standardized form (or checklist) can be helpful, but be certain to tailor it to meet your needs. You may need to address a host of points that are ignored in the standard form you begin with. Meanwhile, completing the tear-out form can help to inform and guide your family, loved ones, and health care providers in making many vital medical decisions. The forms, when properly implemented by a lawyer in your state, will minimize the legal interference and complications of carrying out your end-of-life wishes.

SIGN A HEALTH CARE PROXY IN ADDITION TO A LIVING WILL

You should always sign a health care proxy, even if you have a living will and even if you have trusted loved ones to appoint as agents.

Planning Point: Many experts suggest that the health care proxy be relied on as the primary or sole document for addressing health care and end-of-life decisions because of the uncertainty that many end-of-life medical decisions create. While there is much certainty, many issues are not certain. A religious affiliation is a certainty, and you can state what your beliefs are. If you wish a certain type of funeral, you can state that with certainty. These are not gray areas for which you need an agent with discretion. A living will assumes predominance if you don't have anyone whom you can trust to make the decisions for you. Even if the living will is not the ideal approach and it is rejected in some states, it remains in such situations the only option for communicating your wishes.

In a health care proxy, you appoint someone as your agent to make health care decisions. You need the health care proxy in addition to the living will because a living will does not have sufficient legal recognition in all cases. For example, for a living will to be valid, decisions may have to be made in a manner that presents "clear and convincing" proof of your wishes. General statements such as "no heroic measures," which are typically used in living wills, may not suffice.

You must also sign a health care proxy because it is impossible to conceive of all situations that may occur in a living will so that an agent appointed under your health care proxy can endeavor to fill in the gaps based on the guidelines contained in your living will. Therefore, the safest approach is for you to sign both a living will and a separate health care proxy and have them witnessed and notarized separately (more on how they should be signed later).

UNDERSTANDING THE RELATIONSHIP OF YOUR LIVING WILL AND YOUR HEALTH CARE PROXY

You need a living will to set forth explanations of your general health care wishes. Ideally, your living will can include details of your general health care wishes, as well as more specific end-of-life requests and other important matters. You also need a health care proxy, which is a legal document through which you designate a trusted person (agent) to make health care decisions for you if, because of illness or disability, you are unable to do so yourself. The agent named in your health care proxy should carry out (typically by signing medical decision forms for your health care providers) the wishes you outlined in your living will. Although the two documents are integrally related, having them prepared and executed as independently signed, separate documents may, in some instances, facilitate their use.

Some health care providers prefer a health care proxy so that they can have your named agent execute documents confirming health care decisions. In other situations, a more personalized explanation of your health care wishes, as provided by a living will, may be more appropriate for addressing the situation at hand.

Example: John Smith signed a living will, which included the following clause: "Since ceasing to provide liquids or food inevitably leads to a patient's death, I view this as a form of active euthanasia and direct that my agent shall not authorize it." Months later, John fell gravely ill. The physician is considering inserting a feeding tube and asks the family whether there is a living will. After reading the previous clause, the family splits along the lines of a vicious dispute. Some say that John did not possibly contemplate that a tube would have to be inserted surgically to permit feeding. Others take an opposing view that John would have wanted any form of nutrition and hydration possible. The clause in the living will, while seemingly clear, remains open to interpretation. Either of two possible steps could have resolved the uncertainty; both steps together, however, would be preferable in light of the uncertainty. First, if a health care proxy was signed, it should be up to the agent named to make the decision. In addition, the living will could have added a more detailed provision, including: "Nutrition and hydration shall include, by way of example, and not limitation, tube feedings, Corpak tubes, nasogastric tubes, Levin tubes, gastrostomy tube, or hyperalimentation."

This example illustrates one of the many fundamental types of health care decisions you may wish to have made in a certain manner. Communicating your wishes is the objective of your living will.

Some experts suggest that the difference between your living will and health care proxy is that your living will should address what happens in the event of your imminent death or "point of no return," and your health care proxy should address what should happen if it is more likely that you will survive. This approach and perspective is not recommended and can cause a host of problems. A living will that addresses decisions only when death is imminent may be of no help to your physician in the event of an emergency when your health care agent cannot be reached. Further, as illustrated throughout this book, the determination as to whether survival is expected, and with what state of quality of life, is subjective and not always clear. You'll be much better served by focusing on the definitions and distinctions in this book between the two documents. (Chapter 5 addresses these issues in the context of health care proxies.)

WHY DO YOU NEED A LIVING WILL?

Deciding how you should be cared for in the event of grave illness is an extraordinarily difficult and emotional decision. The importance of making your wishes for health care treatment known if you are unable to communicate your decisions when you are gravely ill has become an integral part of estate and personal planning for every adult. Without advance preparation, your health care and other end-of-life wishes may not be carried out. Your family or loved ones could face gut-wrenching decisions with no solace in knowing what you would have wanted.

Thinking about and discussing terminal illness and death is never a pleasant or easy matter. However, your failure to provide your loved ones with guidance now while you are able to do so may cause them to second guess what you would have wanted done, which is a far more difficult and emotionally traumatic task for them.

Thus, it is essential to communicate guidelines as to how you want to be cared for in the event of a medical emergency or terminal illness. If this communication process is not effected, your family and loved ones, even if they know your feelings, will not have the legal authority to act on them. By not completing this admittedly unpleasant process now, you can create higher costs and unpleasantness for your loved ones.

Your personal goals may be compromised, and your last months or years could be spent in agony or without the minimal quality of life you desire. Your financial and estate planning objectives can be jeopardized when resulting large health care and legal bills deplete your estate. This might be avoided by clarifying your wishes now.

If you do not address living will and related health care issues now, when the time comes to make these difficult decisions, you may not possess the mental capacity to do so. The result may be that doctors, courts, or others may not try to ascertain your wishes and take steps opposite to what you would want. You do not want your personal situation to become another court case in the public eye as the cases in Chapter 1 (and the many more cases not listed there) all sadly became.

USE "CLEAR AND CONVINCING" LANGUAGE IN YOUR LIVING WILL

Your living will should be a clear statement of your health care wishes, your end-of-life decisions, and a few, or perhaps many, related issues that are important to you. General statements, while sometimes helpful, can also be so vague as to create problems. Courts have generally insisted that your wishes be demonstrated by "clear and convincing evidence." The courts want to have some assurance that you really did communicate your health care wishes in a manner that can reasonably be interpreted. Consider the following:

Sample Clause: I authorize my agent to cease heroic medical measures.

Although the term *heroic measures* is commonly used, is it really clear enough to provide any guidance when used in the manner such as in the previous sample clause? If a new experimental procedure becomes available while you are comatose and that procedure has limited scientific support, it is probably pretty clearly "heroic." But if it had a 15 percent chance of curing your disease with only modest side effects, you would likely want it. However, if it is heroic, might you have just directed your medical providers not to use it? Consider an alternative approach:

Sample Clause: I authorize, but do not require, my agent to cease heroic medical measures if I am in a persistent vegetative state or terminally ill and, in my agent's discretion after consultation with my attending physician, the burdens of such care outweigh the benefits it is likely to afford me. In analyzing the benefits, I authorize and direct my agent to consider the effect on my wife.

Although this clause certainly could be clarified and expanded further, it certainly provides substantially more guidance on how a "heroic measure" is to be interpreted and handled. The result could be quite different with the clearer language.

The need for "clear and convincing" statements, with sufficient detail to serve as guidance, relates to all aspects of your living will, not just to the key end-of-life decisions (the "pull the plug" issue that receives all the attention). Suppose you have some limited willingness to be an organ donor, but you sign a standard Internet form, which includes the following clause:

Sample Clause: I authorize my agent to make anatomical gifts (organ donations).

Your agent or a medical provider would likely assume, based on this language, that any of your organs can be donated, and they perhaps might even donate organs to medical schools for research. If what was really meant was something more specific, as described in the following paragraph, the problems with the previous broad phrase become evident. Consider the following clause:

Sample Clause: I authorize my agent to make anatomical gifts (organ donations) that will take effect at my death for the sole purpose of transplant to save the life of a member of my family, but for no other purpose and in no other circumstance.

Detail that is personalized and specific to your circumstances is the goal you should strive for.

COMPREHENSIVE FORM AND APPROACH

The approach presented in this discussion and contained in more detailed form in Chapter 3 is more comprehensive than what is provided in many of the commercial forms you can purchase on the Internet or in office supply stores or obtain from various organizations. Often the commercial forms are limited to simple instructions such as "pulling the plug" in the event of a terminal illness. There is a broad range of health care and related medical issues that should be addressed to ensure you and your loved ones adequate protection. This discussion and the examples explain many of the issues you might wish to address.

Many of the simple commercial forms simply do not provide an adequate means for you to communicate your wishes to friends, family, or others you will rely on. Most importantly, the form you use must address your personal needs and concerns and not simply be a generic approach. Your personal preferences, religious concerns, family, and other personal relationships should all be considered.

PAIN RELIEF

Pain relief is very important to address in your living will. A number of perspectives should be communicated to your caregivers:

- Clarity of mind may be impaired: Pain relief may be very desirable, but at what cost and when?

Case Studies

Having sat at the bedside of many clients struggling through their last weeks and days, we see a common thread. Almost all people, if they haven't previously addressed it, want to put their lives in order. It might consist of signing a will, writing a letter of last instruction, or saying personal goodbyes. One client, Hedy, struggled and put off taking pain medication to remain lucid enough to plan for her husband's financial security. A close friend, Saul, told nurses on several occasions to come back later with pain medication so he could focus on getting his affairs in order, signing a will, and planning for the college education of his beloved nieces and nephews.

In the previous examples, and scores of other circumstances, simply providing maximum pain relief, something most would quickly state they want, would deny many people the ability to complete their affairs and hence squelch this common end-of-life process.

- *Pain relief may hasten death.* What about pain medication and other treatments or procedures to reduce pain? Should they be administered even if they hasten death? Should a distinction be made between the side effect of pain relief somewhat hastening death and affirmatively using pain medication in doses intended to cause death? How can this distinction be made? Providing some guidance in your living will for these gray areas could be very important.
- *Religious beliefs may be violated.* Pain relief has a number of important religious implications. For many, some lucidity at or near the end of life is vital to carry out important religious functions (see Chapter 4). Providing pain relief that dulls the senses or makes you unaware may deny you the ability to participate in important rituals. Are there any adverse religious implications if pain relief hastens death?
- *Pain relief might be inadequate.* Some patients who are unable to communicate have been denied adequate pain relief. Lawsuits have been filed against health care providers for not providing adequate pain relief. Specify what your desires are in your living will.

NO HEROIC MEASURES OR ALL MEASURES

Should mechanical means of prolonging life be used? One difficulty is that it is impossible to know which treatments will be necessary or available. How do you define *heroic?* What is heroic in one situation may not be heroic in another. Some forms are specific, providing a complex grid of boxes to check off types of medical procedures you want or do not want, based on various hypothetical scenarios. But what happens if your scenario is a little different from what's in the boxes? Now what do they do? It's worse than having nothing. Chapter 4 discusses many sample provisions that you can review with your health care provider (and clergy if applicable). As illustrated in an earlier example in this chapter, should the benefits and burdens of particular medical procedures be evaluated in addition to the heroic nature of those procedures? Would you really want to avoid the most heroic procedure if there is any chance of cure and little likelihood of pain? What does *cure* mean? If you remain in a vegetative state, is it worth curing your illness that would have caused death? Or is the "benefit" of living in a persistent vegetative state not worthwhile? What does *heroic* mean to you and under what circumstances?

With so much press and attention given to the right to die, euthanasia, cessation of medical procedures, and related issues, one very important fact has been obscured. You may want every medically reasonable method, heroic or not, performed. If you want every life-saving procedure and extraordinary measure performed (e.g., cardiac resuscitation, mechanical respiration, nutrition, hydration), your living will should state this.

NUTRITION AND HYDRATION

You should specifically state whether you would permit your agent to ever withdraw artificial nutrition and hydration. If you do not wish to have artificial feeding, even if discontinuing it could hasten death, this should be specifically stated. Many states do not permit the cessation of nutrition or hydration unless the form specifically authorizes it. Some states require that if your health care proxy is to permit the agent to withdraw nutrition or hydration, the form must be separately signed beside that provision. How should *artificial* be defined?

Should a distinction be made between withdrawing nutrition and hydration (e.g., a feeding tube) versus withholding the initial connection to artificial feeding tubes? Do your religious beliefs affect this decision? Many view nutrition and hydration as mere palliative care, not medical care. According to this view, nutrition and hydration should always be given and never withdrawn. Is this your view? Because of this fundamental issue as to what "nutrition and hydration" are, you need to expressly address them in your living will.

QUALITY-OF-LIFE STATEMENTS

Your living will may be the only written evidence of your deepest personal wishes. Therefore, it should as clearly and as precisely as possible state your feelings and wishes about health care, treatment, quality of life, whether you wish to refuse or accept medical treatment, and so forth. The law may require that the living will demonstrate this with "clear and convincing evidence." Many living wills contain general statements that if there is "no quality of life," then "no heroic measures" should be taken to prolong your life. "No quality of life" might mean to one person the inability to communicate to the outside world, with no anticipation of recovery. To another person, "no quality of life" might mean severe and ongoing pain that cannot be abated. Religious beliefs preclude some people from addressing quality-of-life issues because life itself is viewed as so sacred. Perhaps there is no single issue that creates more controversy, uncertainty, and difficulty than defining quality of life.

Personal Case Study

The following is an essay written by my stepson recounting his perceptions of his grandmother's end-of-life decision when he was a young teen. His compassionate, articulate, and insightful perspective of a difficult and traumatic time demonstrates how addressing quality-of-life decisions can be done with dignity and in a manner that enhances the experience for all involved. Whether you agree with the decision made or how it was handled, there are many valuable insights and lessons to be learned.

"Perhaps the most significant experience that I have had to face in recent years was the death of my grandma. At the age of 14, this was the first time where I had to deal with the loss of someone very close to me. However, it was not the painful experience that most people would associate with the death of a family member. Instead, it was a unique learning experience for me personally and for my entire family. I consider this experience unique because our family had the chance to say good-bye to our grandmother.

In mid-September of 2000, my grandmother's condition was deteriorating after complications following a surgical procedure. My grandma had kidney failure in an operation several years before, and since then she had needed dialysis treatment several times each week. When she received her dialysis treatment for the first time after the operation, she began to feel a tingling sensation in her legs. Later that afternoon, she was paralyzed from the waist down.

Of course, the news came as a complete shock. I knew my grandma had not been in the greatest health, but this seemed like a crushing blow. A day or two after I heard this news, I left home on a school trip with the freshman class of my high school to Frost Valley, a YMCA camp in upstate New York. Frost Valley has various educational outdoor activities, such as hiking trails and a ropes course. The trip was meant to introduce us to our classmates and help us bond together as a class. I was attending a public magnet high school, so most of my classmates were merely my acquaintances only three weeks into the school year. Although I did make friends over the trip, I was somewhat distracted since my thoughts were with my grandma at home.

After every meal during the three days we spent at Frost Valley, one of the staff members shared an inspirational quote. While many of the students scoffed at the quotes, believing that they were corny or stupid, I quietly enjoyed them for their insight. One quote that was shared at our last meal on the trip stood out from all the others: 'Don't cry because it is over; smile because it happened.'

When I returned home after the class trip, my father explained to me that my grandma decided to voluntarily withdraw from dialysis treatment. He explained that she would not be able to live without the treatment, and she would pass away three to four days after she received her last treatment. Each day after school, my parents brought me to the hospital so I could spend time with my grandma.

Because she had been on dialysis and had a history of kidney problems, she had been on a very restrictive diet for the last several years of her life. However, in this week—the last week of her life—I watched her eat the foods that she had not been able to eat for the last 10 years. I watched the joy on her face as she ate Chinese food for lunch one day, a roast beef sandwich at another meal, and simply a bagel with cream cheese for a breakfast. Although she did not have much of an appetite, she drew much pleasure from living life in a way she had not been able to live for years. It was very satisfying to watch her enjoy the simple pleasures in life that I had taken for granted.

On a Sunday, the entire extended family came to visit my grandma. They were bracing for a difficult day of tears and grief, but they were caught completely by surprise. My grandma was telling jokes, laughing, telling stories—it was hard to tell that she was living her final days. I think the family almost felt guilty for enjoying themselves on a day that was supposed to be very difficult. On that day, my grandma called all the family members in one by one for a personal goodbye. It was humorous in a way; she was taking complete control, telling each family member who should be sent in to say goodbye next.

In her conversation with me, she explained that there is such a thing as quality of life, and she decided that she did not wish to finish her life paralyzed, restricted to a chair or bed. She taught me that I should enjoy life to its fullest and that I should enjoy everything that comes out of living. I learned that life truly is a gift. As she spoke with me in private for what would be the last time, I remembered the quote I heard at Frost Valley, and I thought it was very appropriate for the situation. I whispered in her ear, 'Don't cry because it is over; smile because it happened.' She smiled, and we said our final goodbye.

My grandma died on Thursday, September 28. In the Jewish faith, after the passing of a loved one, the immediate family begins a mourning period of seven days. The observation of this mourning period is known as 'sitting Shiva.' On this year, however, Rosh Hashanah, the joyous holiday of the Jewish New Year, began the following day at sundown. This had an interesting implication on the mourning period following death. Effectively, the mourning period is cancelled as soon as Rosh Hashanah begins since the New Year is meant to be a joyous occasion. Our family agreed that this is what our grandma would have wanted. She did not want us to mourn her passing, but instead for us to get on with our lives, enjoying every moment."

You should analyze your own feelings and concerns about quality of life. If this concept is important to your determination as to whether life support should be halted, be sure to modify the document accordingly to reflect your wishes. You may wish to add personal feelings or comments to tailor the appropriate portions of your living will document.

ANATOMICAL GIFTS (ORGAN DONATIONS)

Organ donations are a vital step to help save the lives of others. Seriously and carefully give thought to permitting organ donations. Before rejecting the idea of being an organ donor, you should at least give careful consideration to the ramifications, the thousands of people who die each year awaiting organ transplants, and the great good you can accomplish by being a donor.

If you want to limit the transplant to life-saving situations only or limit potential donees to family only, you should so specify.

Can organ or tissue donations be used for more than mere transplant? This should be specified. Are organs donated to be used only for medical study or education, or are the organs and/or tissues donated to be restricted in some way? Do you wish to specify limitations or permit gifts in accordance with your religious preferences?

If you wish to be an organ donor and have any religious affiliations, carefully consult with your religious adviser concerning organ donations generally, and in particular for other than transplant to save lives. Some religious interpretations may restrict transplant to preservation of life situations only. Do not dismiss organ donations for religious reasons alone unless you have consulted your religious adviser. Many people erroneously assume that organ donations are prohibited for religious reasons. How and under what circumstances specific organs can be donated may be subject to some restrictions, but often they are not generally prohibited.

If you still feel uncomfortable permitting organ donation, consider instead restricting the provision. Would you refuse organ donations to save the life of a family member?

BURIAL INSTRUCTIONS

If you wish any specific eulogy, service, or procedures, specify it in your living will. If you want a traditional religious ceremony, say so. You can also specify that religious restrictions do not apply but that burial should be in accordance with a particular religion's traditions. You may wish to specify cremation and interment instead of burial. You can note detailed burial instructions in your living will. Alternatively, you can instead communicate these desires in a letter of last instructions. Consider, however, including certain minimum statements in your living will. State also whether you do or do not wish a ceremony in accordance with a particular religious preference.

Case Study

We have to hide most of the facts of this case because it was an ugly and painful event. The client had passed away, and her surviving husband planned the funeral service as they had discussed and agreed on. One of their sons had in the prior few years become very religious. Although the family remained loyal to their religious roots, they did not practice or observe. As a result, many aspects of the funeral service deviated from what their religious traditions would have mandated. The son, dogmatic in his newfound beliefs and wishing what he thought respectful and appropriate for his deceased mother, created a fight and a traumatic scene at the funeral. The father later signed a living will and health care proxy. In his living will, he provided express and detailed provisions of what he wanted for his funeral service. In his health care proxy, he expressly stated that his son should not participate in any decision making. Although these steps may not prevent an emotional outburst at the father's funeral, they certainly communicate clearly what his wishes are.

If you wish to be cremated, state this. If you don't want cremation and you are concerned that someone might believe you do, you need to state that as well.

Depending on your family and personal situation, you might wish to provide some instruction as to who should or should not speak at your funeral service, where you want to be buried or interred, and any other matters that might be problematic for those surviving.

COMMON PRACTICAL ISSUES AFFECTING YOUR LIVING WILL

Will Ambulance and Emergency Medical Technicians Accept a Living Will?

Ambulance and emergency medical technicians have as their primary goal saving lives—keeping the patient alive until he or she reaches a hospital. The urgent nature of their activities, the time frame of their involvement, and their primary mission make it difficult, if not impossible, for them to review, interpret, and then apply the provisions of a living will. Plan in advance. If you are terminally ill and spending your last days at home, perhaps you should instruct your family and loved ones not to call an ambulance but rather call the hospice or simply take you to the hospital by taxi. Consider alternative transportation arrangements to the hospital to avoid the issue of receiving heroic measures in the ambulance. Discuss this with your doctor in advance.

What Should You Do with Your Old Living Wills?

Most living wills should include a provision revoking prior living wills. If yours doesn't, you might want to have your attorney add such a clause when you next revise it. This clause means that any living will with an earlier date is invalid. However, if someone in an emergency finds the older living will and not the current one, he or she may have no way of knowing that you have signed a new living will. Therefore, it is always best to locate and destroy old living wills—originals and copies—especially if you have made significant changes in your wishes.

Consider the Policies of Health Care Facilities

If you are going to enter a hospital, nursing facility, or other health care facility, be certain to review its policies toward fundamental health care issues. If the organization's policies are incompatible with your health care wishes, you may wish to evaluate alternative facilities. For example, if the facility has a religious affiliation or religious sponsoring organization, there may be a strict policy against assisted suicide or euthanasia. This policy may not be changed regardless of what is stated in your living will. A health care facility with religious affiliations may have a policy of administering nutrition and hydration unless medically contraindicated. If you are a Jehovah's Witness and wish to avoid blood transfusions, you should endeavor to identify in advance hospitals that can better meet your needs. If you have chosen a particular course of action in your living will, you may need to select in advance the medical facility with similar care.

How Many Living Wills Should You Sign?

There are different views concerning how many original living wills you can sign. Some experts suggest signing only one and then making copies. If this approach is taken, be certain that your living will expressly authorizes the making and distribution of copies. Other experts prefer to sign multiple original living wills so in an emergency an original will be available. You should retain an original at home (not in a safe deposit box or vault where it is inaccessible in an emergency). Give your agent an original to hold. This procedure will ensure that the agent will be aware of his or her role and have an original document to give your medical care providers to copy for inclusion in your medical records. In an emergency, you very likely may not have the presence of mind or ability to take your living will with you, so giving your agent an original in advance is a good safety precaution. Finally, your attorney who helped draft your living will should retain an original. Often, in an emergency, family members call the attorney if they cannot locate the original.

STEPS YOU SHOULD TAKE CONCERNING YOUR LIVING WILL

Discuss Your Living Will with Family, Friends, and Loved Ones

As important as the document you sign is the process through which you determine what your living will should contain. The process should include discussions about your feelings with your family, doctor, and religious adviser, if applicable. All may be involved in the decisions concerning your health care should you ever be unable to express your own wishes. They cannot be expected to advise your health care agent as to how to carry out your desires without your having first informed them of your feelings. The more openly you discuss your feelings with family, the more likely that you can ease the burden of the decisions they could face.

While your religious adviser can assist your doctors and family in reaching a decision that is in accordance with applicable religious tenants and your personal beliefs, an awareness of your feelings can be important in properly guiding your family and physicians. The process of communicating your beliefs and feelings is one of the most important steps, and this can't be done by signing a quick-fix form from the Internet or even a boilerplate form with your lawyer.

Read Your State's Living Will Law

Even if you hire an estate planning specialist in your state to review and guide you on the final preparation (drafting) and signing (execution) of your living will, which is recommended, you should take the time to read your state's law (statute) covering (governing) living wills. The law is unlikely to be long, and reading it will give you a much better understanding of what is involved, what issues you should address in your living will, and how gaps in your living will might be interpreted or filled in by your state's law. State statute books are readily available at most public libraries, and your librarian can direct you. If you use this approach, be sure to look at not only the relevant sections of the law in the book, but also any amendments to the law, which are often contained in a pamphlet at the back of the book (called a "pocket part"). The easiest way to identify your state statutes is on the Internet. A simple search should do it.

The recommendation to review your state's health care proxy law is discussed in Chapter 5.

STATE LIVING WILL LAWS

State Name	Law (Statute) Reference	Specific Sections (§§) of the Law
Alabama	Alabama Code	22-8A-1 to 22-8A-10
Alaska	Alaska Statute	18.12.010 to 18.12.100
Arizona	Arizona Revised Statute Annotated	36-3201 et seq.
Arkansas	Arkansas Code Annotated	20-17-201 to 20-17-218
California	Health and Safety Code	7186.5
Colorado	Colorado Revised Statute	15-18-101 to 15-18-113
Connecticut	Connecticut General Statute	19A-570 to 19A-580c
Delaware	Delaware Code Annotated Title 16	2503 to 2509
District of Columbia	District of Columbia Code Annotated	21-2201 to 21-2213
Florida	Florida Statute Chapter	765.301 et seq.
Georgia	Georgia Code Annotated	31-32-1 to 31-32-12
Hawaii	Hawaii Revised Statute	327D-1 et seq.
Idaho	Idaho Code	39-4501 to 39-4509
Illinois	Illinois Revised Statute	755 et seq.
Indiana	Indiana Code	16-36-4-1 to 16-36-4-21
Iowa	Iowa Code	144A.1 et seq.
Kansas	Kansas Statute Annotated	65-28, 101 et seq.
Kentucky	Kentucky Revised Statute Annotated	311.621 to 311.643
Louisiana	Louisiana Revised Statute Annotated	40:1299.58.1 et seq.
Maine	Maine Revised Statute Annotated Title 18-A	5-701 et seq.
Maryland	Maryland Code Annotated, Health-General	5-601 to 5-618
Massachusetts	Massachusetts General Law Chapter 201D	1 et seq.
Michigan	Michigan Compilation Laws	700.496 et seq.
Minnesota	Minnesota Statute	145B.01 et seq.
Mississippi	Mississippi Code Annotated	41-41-1511 et seq.
Missouri	Missouri Revised Statute	459.010 et seq.
Montana	Montana Code Annotated	50-9-101 et seq.
Nebraska	Nebraska Revised Statute	20-401 et seq.

(continued)

State Name	Law (Statute) Reference	Specific Sections (§§) of the Law
Nevada	Nevada Revised Statute	449.535-690 and 449.800-860
New Hampshire	New Hampshire Revised Statute Annotated	137-H:1 et seq.
New Jersey	New Jersey Revised Statute	26:2H-53
New Mexico	New Mexico Statute Annotated	24-7-1 to 24-7-10
New York	New York Public Health Law	2980 et seq.
North Carolina	North Carolina General Statute	90-320 to 90-332
North Dakota	North Dakota Central Code	23-06.4-01 to 23-06.4-14
Ohio	Ohio Revised Code Annotated	4506.01 et seq.
Oklahoma	Oklahoma Statute Title 63	3101-4 et seq.
Oregon	Oregon Revised Statute	127.505 et seq.
Pennsylvania	20 Pennsylvania Conn. Statute Annotated	540 et seq.
Rhode Island	Rhode Island General Laws	23-4.11-1 to 23-4.11-14
South Carolina	South Carolina Code Annotated	44-66-10 et seq.
South Dakota	South Dakota Codified Laws Annotated	34-12D-1 to 34-12D-22
Tennessee	Tennessee Code Annotated	32-11-1-1 et seq.
Texas	Texas Health And Safety Code Annotated	672.001 et seq.
Utah	Utah Code Annotated	75-2-1101 et seq.
Vermont	Vermont Statute Annotated Title 18	5251 et seq.
Virginia	Virginia Code Annotated	54.1-2981 to 54.1-2993
Washington	Washington Revised Code	70.122.010 et seq.
West Virginia	West Virginia Code	16-30-1 16-30C-1 et seq.
Wisconsin	Wisconsin Statute	154.01 et seq.
Wyoming	Wyoming Statute	35-22-100

Coordinate Your Durable Power of Attorney for Financial Matters

A durable power of attorney with financial powers is an integral part of your overall health care and estate planning (see Chapter 10). If the agent you authorize to carry out your health care wishes does not have the financial wherewithal or the legal access to your funds to carry out your health care wishes, your desires could also be stymied. This issue should be addressed in a separate document focused on financial matters and never as part of a living will (or health care proxy), which should be limited to personal, end-of-life, and health care matters. Designating someone to handle financial matters that will respect your health care agent's decisions can be particularly important when your attitude about the implications of a living will or health care proxy differ from attitudes of family members. If your living will specifies that you would want palliative hospice care, but your financial agent has strong moral convictions that all life must be preserved, will the financial agent refuse to pay for the palliative care you want, which you specified in your living will and which your health care agent authorized?

As an alternative, a living trust (not to be confused with a living will), which is also called a *revocable inter vivos trust*, can be used. When properly prepared, this trust can be a much more comprehensive document addressing a broad range of financial and other issues, including the handling of your financial matters in the event of disability. The revocable living trust remains a powerful and flexible planning tool for handling your financial matters in the event of disability, including your inability to make financial and related decisions as a result of illness or injury (see Chapter 10).

Carry a Pocket Card

Whatever your wishes concerning your health care, properly prepared documents are far too bulky to carry on your person.

In an emergency situation, your attending physicians can at least be informed by a wallet card indicating that you signed a living will and health care proxy and whom to contact. It might also specify a major term of your living will: "No heroic measures." "All medically appropriate procedures requested." "No heroic measures in accordance with Catholic religious principles." A quick and succinct notice on a pocket card can be invaluable in an emergency.

QUESTIONS TO CONSIDER

1. If you are unable to make health care decisions for yourself, who would you feel comfortable with to make those important decisions for you? Who should be your health care agent? Who should serve if your first agent cannot?

2. Would the person you choose feel comfortable making those decisions for you? Would he or she have the presence of mind and ability to do so?

3. Is quality of life relevant to the end-of-life medical care you would wish to have? If so, would you want efforts made to try to save or improve your condition if it meant you would be wheelchair bound for the remainder of your life? What if you were to be bedridden? If you are likely to be in constant physical pain and anguish, would your opinion change? What if you can only be sustained on a feeding tube? How would the necessity of your being hooked up to a machine to feed you or keep you alive affect your view? Would you prefer to live in a nursing home if you were unable to care for yourself?

4. Would you want your organs to be donated? Should they be donated only to save another life? What if they could be used for educational purposes?

5. Where and how do you want to be buried? Do you desire any particular type of funeral service?

6. Do you want to have your remains cremated? If so, where should the ashes be interred?

CHAPTER SUMMARY

When planning your end-of-life decisions, both a living will and a health care proxy are important. The living will sets forth your directives on a broad range of issues; that is, which life saving procedures to apply, if any; what to do with your organs upon death; and what to do with your body after death. The health care proxy appoints an agent to make decisions on your behalf if you are unable to make them. No two people have exactly the same views, feelings, wishes, or concerns. This chapter has discussed many of the fundamental issues to consider for your living will. Tailoring and refining these fundamental decisions will set the stage for you to address the more specific issues discussed in Chapter 3 and help assure that your documents and planning address your wishes.

3 DETAILED LIVING WILL ISSUES YOU MUST CONSIDER

INTRODUCTION TO YOUR LIVING WILL DECISIONS AND DRAFTING

The culmination of your analysis of living will decisions and of the discussions with family and advisers is a living will legal document, which you can sign under the supervision of your attorney. This chapter follows the sequence of provisions in the sample tear-out living will form provided in Chapter 11 to help you understand the provisions of the sample living will form and give you guidance in making the difficult and complex decisions that are necessary to complete the sample form. Once you've made the decisions discussed in this chapter, you can complete the tear-out form and take it to your lawyer for review and formal signing (execution).

INTRODUCTORY PARAGRAPHS OF YOUR LIVING WILL

The initial paragraphs of your living will can vary considerably, depending on the form you use, your state, and your fundamental preferences (see Chapter 2). Some common themes should be considered.

These introductory paragraphs of your living will should specify that you are competent to understand and sign the document. Your competence is essential to the fundamental concept of your consent for certain medical treatment to be given, withheld, or withdrawn. The key to ensuring that a living will is respected as a representation of "clear and convincing" evidence of your wishes if you are later unable to communicate is that you were competent when you signed it. To achieve this result, your living will might confirm that you are an adult (over the age of majority in your state). A living will signed as a minor will not be legally valid, although it still might be considered by those trying to understand your wishes. Thus, if you are a minor afflicted with a particular illness or have suffered a serious debilitating injury, you might still prepare and sign a living will to formally communicate how you feel.

The living will should state that you are of sound mind, and otherwise capable of making the decisions reflected in your living will. The witnesses to your living will should be able to confirm your statement (see later discussion). If you are in questionable health when you sign your living will, you might wish to take the additional steps of having a physician certify in writing that you are competent to sign the living will.

The introductory provisions in your living will could include a statement that you are, by signing the living will, exercising your fundamental right to make voluntary, informed choices to accept, reject, or choose among alternative courses of medical and surgical treatment. The document might also state that you are making the declarations (statements) contained in your living will as a directive to be followed if for any reason you later become incapacitated or incompetent and are thus unable to participate in decisions about medical care. Your living will recognizes that a time may come when you cannot participate in your medical care decisions, regardless of the favorable prospect for recovery, and may include statements to this effect. Again, the purpose is to state that your living will should be a statement to stand as an expression of your wishes, beliefs, objectives, and directions for care.

Because it is not possible for you to anticipate the diverse medical decisions that may have to be made in the future and give specific written directions at the time of signing your living will, you should appoint an agent to make specific decisions when necessary, in accordance with your wishes. Your living will should include an acknowledgment to make it clear to anyone reading it that your statements are guidance, but that your agent will have the power to make decisions necessary to implement your general guidance and wishes.

The introductory paragraphs may also provide an overview of why you are signing the living will. For example, note any specific religious or moral preference prominently at the beginning of the form so it is quickly apparent to anyone in an emergency.

Many living wills include several general statements in the introductory paragraphs. In most cases, your living will should be provided to your medical care providers for inclusion in your patient chart. Many forms include an express statement to this effect: "I direct that this living will become a part of my permanent medical records."

Often, it is not only medical care providers involved in implementing your end-of-life wishes. You should, therefore, direct in your living will your intent that the actions of your family, friends, clergymen, physicians, nurses, and all those concerned with your care proceed as provided in your living will.

No one wishes to put himself or herself or loved ones through the media exposure many key end-of-life cases have created. While there can be no assurance that media exposure can be avoided, you can express your hope that your end-of-life wishes be honored by health care facilities, physicians, and families without having to go through the process of any judicial or other determination.

VISITATION AND PARTICIPATION BY YOUR SPOUSE OR PARTNER

Although the Cleaver family is a rare occurrence in today's hybrid, blended, politically correct, social environment, life still seems to be based on the June and Ward Cleaver model as the norm. If you are in a nonmarital partnership relationship, your living relationship and your partner should be given the same courtesy as a marital relationship. While the most important step to ensure this courtesy is naming your partner as your agent under your health care proxy, you should also state your wishes in your living will. For example, your living will could state that for purposes of visitation in hospitals, nursing homes, or other facilities, it is your wish that your partner be treated and considered for all purposes as an immediate family member or spouse and be given the widest latitude and accommodation as if a member of your immediate family or spouse.

SHOULD YOUR LIVING WILL ALSO NAME A PERSON TO ACT IF YOU CANNOT (AGENT)?

You will need to appoint an attorney-in-fact as well as an agent and successor agents to represent your wishes in the event you are unable to make the decisions yourself. The primary document to do this is the health care power of attorney (also called *health care proxy*). Some experts recommend that the same persons be listed in your living will and empowered to implement the wishes discussed in your health care proxy. The purpose of this dual appointment is to ensure that if someone is considering only your living will or has access to only your living will, the document independent of your health care proxy will create a basis for action. When this dual approach (i.e., designating agents in both your living will and health care proxy) is used, you must ensure that the same people are named in the same order in both documents or you will create a conflict that might invalidate both documents. When this dual approach is used, your health care proxy still includes a detailed list of powers your agent is given, which your living will should not. Your living will would still include descriptions of your health care and other end-of-life wishes, which your health care proxy would not. A detailed discussion of how to name an agent, whom to name, and how to appoint him or her, is included in the discussion of heath care proxies in Chapter 5.

GENERAL STATEMENT OF YOUR HEALTH CARE WISHES

The single most important concept to address in your living will is a general explanation of what health care philosophy you wish followed if you are unable to make your own decisions. You need to address the scope of if, when, and to what extent medical care should be continued, withheld, or withdrawn. Unless you are aware of a particular severe medical issue when you are preparing your living will, it is highly unlikely that you can anticipate eventualities; and even if facing a specific disease, the myriad complications, conditions, and other variables make explicit determinations in advance impossible. There are, however, a number of macro or general parameters that you can address in your living will, which can provide tremendous guidance. The following key questions will help you formulate these guiding provisions:

- Do you believe that quality of life is a factor that should be considered in deciding whether a particular medical treatment should be pursued? If so, how do you define quality of life?
- If you have a terminal illness that, in all likelihood, will result in your death in, for example, three months, should you be revived or treated for another illness or complication that may shorten your life? Answer the same question for one week, six months, and one year. Answer the question assuming you were able to communicate with others during this time period and again assuming you were not able to communicate.
- Do you believe all life is sacred and that your physical life should be maintained in all circumstances?
- Do you have a predominant religious belief that dictates health care decisions that should serve as a guiding point of this discussion?

Weigh the Benefits and Burdens of Medical Care Decisions

If a particular medical procedure or treatment has a limited potential to alleviate a particular discomfort or problem, but not cure the underlying terminal condition, should it be considered? What if there is a small percentage likelihood of curing your underlying medical condition? What does "benefit" mean to you? If you will in all likelihood remain in a vegetative state, is it worth curing an acute condition that would have otherwise caused an earlier death? Or is the "benefit" of living in a persistent vegetative state not worthwhile? What does "heroic measures" mean to you and under what circumstances?

Should the benefits and burdens of particular medical procedures be evaluated in addition to the heroic nature of those procedures? Would you really want to avoid the most extreme or heroic procedure if there is any chance for that procedure to treat your underlying condition? Should that answer depend on whether there is a likelihood of pain, complications, or other "burdens" of the procedure? What consequences would you consider "burdens"? Should health care providers consider the burdens on your loved ones or only the burdens on you?

Case Study

Eddie, a healthy and dynamic middle-age man, does not want to put his wife through unnecessary suffering. If he is in a persistent vegetative state or has a terminal illness, his living will expressly directs his agent to consider the impact of any decision on his wife. The decision to continue his life support should expressly take into account the impact on her.

No Heroic Medical Efforts Should Be Taken under Specified Conditions

Most people have a general sense that if there is no hope of recovery from a painful terminal illness or they are in a persistent vegetative state, heroic medical measures should not be performed. What most people have in mind is someone with no consciousness or ability to communicate, hooked up to a maze of wire and machines. The reality can be quite different from this Orwellian image, and the language included in many forms is far from what is necessary. Whatever language you consider, you have to understand the implications of what is said, and consider various options in light of your personal preferences, religious concerns, and so on.

A typical approach in a form living will might provide that if you have any of certain specified conditions, heroic measures need not be taken. Several steps of decisions must be made:

Step 1—Severe condition: Determine that you have a severe condition, perhaps by characterizing your condition as one of the following situations:

- An incurable or irreversible, severe mental, or severe physical condition, coordinated with any statements you make concerning your desire for a quality of life.
- In a state of permanent unconsciousness or profound dementia. "Permanently unconscious" should be defined in your living will to avoid differences or uncertainty as to how you would define the concept. It might be defined as a state that, to a reasonable degree of medical certainty, an attending physician certifies in writing that you are irreversibly unaware of yourself and your circumstances and environment, and there is a total loss of cerebral cortical functioning resulting in not having the capacity to experience pain.
- A severe injury. The severity and its implications to your quality of life might warrant discussion in your living will.
- A terminal illness. The term "terminal illness" should be defined in your living will since a significant range of definitions could be applied. Some might define terminal illness as an irreversible, incurable, and untreatable condition caused by disease, illness, or injury when an attending physician can certify in writing that, to a reasonable degree of medical certainty, there is no hope of recovery, or death is likely to occur in a brief period of time if life-sustaining treatment is not provided.

Step 2—No likelihood of recovery: A severe condition alone is not enough to justify cessation of life support or your forgoing a medical treatment. Therefore, in addition to your being in one of the severe situations discussed in Step 1, there should be no reasonable expectation of recovering from such severe, permanent condition and regaining any meaningful quality of life. Many people require that the severe condition prevent them from having any consciousness or if they have consciousness, they must be in severe chronic pain that cannot be properly treated before the cessation of medical care provisions are triggered.

Step 3—No quality of life: Quality of life is of tremendous importance to many people thinking through the health care and end-of-life decisions contained in a living will and in determining the scope and extent of health care services they may wish to have given. Maintaining your life as a mere biological existence, in a vegetative state, may not be an acceptable goal of your medical treatment. If this is your view (and you must clearly state your view) and if there is no reasonable probability that any particular medical treatment would benefit you (your living will must define *benefit*), you may then direct that medical treatments be withheld and withdrawn. If this is not your view (e.g., because of moral, religious, or other reasons) you must expressly say so.

Step 4—Define quality of life: If you meet the conditions set forth in the preceding steps, you might determine and state in your living will that it is your wish that *heroic life-sustaining procedures* and *extraordinary maintenance or medical treatment* be withheld and withdrawn. Because these key terms remain vague and nondescript in spite of their common usage, your living will should elaborate on their meaning. Definitions of these terms should not be dismissed as standard or boilerplate. You should review and tailor them to reflect your beliefs and wishes.

For example, it may not be your desire to prolong your life through mechanical means (e.g., a respirator) where your body is no longer able to perform vital bodily functions on its own and where there is little likelihood of ever regaining any meaningful quality of life. The quality-of-life component may be important for you to address as well. The mere fact that your body will never regain certain functions may be irrelevant if those functions can be performed mechanically and you can still have some quality of life. But what is quality of life to you? It is a very subjective determination. You might define it as returning you to a level of functioning or existence where you could communicate with your loved ones and reasonably understand their communications. Alternatively, you might define it as having mobility, being able to feed yourself, or whatever personal quality-of-life actions are essential to your view of life.

The condition and degree of severity and permanence contemplated by the provisions you include in your living will should be explained. You might state, for example, that if your condition is of such a nature and degree of permanence and is accompanied by so much pain that the average person might contemplate the withdrawal of life support in similar situations, you would not be considered to have a quality of life that would warrant giving, or continuing, life support (or heroic measures).

Step 5—Define "heroic measures": Most people would define "heroic measures" as procedures that are invasive, disruptive of life, and extreme in their effect. Heroic measures are often defined to include procedures and treatments such as surgery, antibiotics, cardiac and pulmonary resuscitation, ventilation, intubation or other respiratory support, medical and surgical tests and treatments, medications, and diagnostic tests of any nature when a person is in one of the conditions described in the previous steps. The determination of what is heroic must, therefore, vary depending on other circumstances. Examples of patients with respiratory problems follow; analyzed from a general perspective and from a religious perspective.

Example: An elderly man suffering with diabetes, kidney failure, heart failure, and Alzheimer's dementia is hospitalized having just suffered a stroke. He becomes short of breath. It is discovered that he has a pulmonary embolus (blood clot in the lungs). He cannot maintain adequate oxygenation. The patient cannot be given anticoagulants (blood thinners) because of the stroke, so, instead, an intravenous filter may be inserted surgically to prevent further clots from reaching his lungs. The issue is how much more invasive or aggressive should treatment be? Should he be intubated? Should he be put on life support and have a ventilator breathe for him? Alternatively, do you let nature take its course at that point? Many people would view intubation of this patient as a heroic measure under these circumstances.

Example: Assume the same facts as in the preceding example but with a different perspective. Some people with a religious worldview or even a different moral perspective might in contrast insist on all life support being given to the patient. They might insist that life support is ethically appropriate since the elderly man is clearly alive, his life can probably be extended, and there may not be significant risks to the intubation. This conclusion may not be fully true, however. The breathing tube can damage the trachea; the patient becomes more susceptible to pneumonia. If intubation is performed, will he ever be able to be removed from the ventilator? For many, once hooked up to the ventilator, removal is more problematic from an ethical perspective because they may view removal as directly causing his death. The patient may have to spend the rest of his life on a ventilator. An endotracheal tube (from the mouth to the lungs) can stay inserted only about 10 days to two weeks. At that point, a tracheotomy must be completed: A surgical incision is made into the windpipe and a tube inserted, which is then attached to the ventilator. With this tube in place, sedation is usually continued because an awake person on a ventilator is very uncomfortable. Talking becomes impossible. If the elderly man is alert, he can make hand motions or write, but a patient in the condition of this example is unlikely to be alert. If the patient has to stay on a ventilator for a long time period, the withdrawal of the ventilator will become more difficult to achieve safely because the respiratory muscles weaken with prolonged ventilation. Is this really the right approach? Do the family members (or the man's agent under his health care proxy) understand the full consequences of ordering the mechanical ventilation?

Example: A 38-year-old woman, who is active and generally in good health, after a long, direct airplane flight from Asia to the United States suffers a pulmonary embolus (blood clot in the lung). The patient would likely be given anticoagulants (blood thinners) instead of the more invasive insertion of an intervenous filter as in the elderly man's case and should clearly be intubated if she is short of breath and unable to maintain adequate oxygenation. Intubating such a patient is unlikely to be viewed as heroic. Once this otherwise healthy young patient is on a ventilator and the pulmonary embolus is dealt with, she can probably be weaned from the ventilator and will likely return to a full and normal life.

If the living wills for both of these people say that heroic measures need not be taken, how will they be distinguished in practice? One method of distinguishing the determination of what is heroic in these two different circumstances is the use of a health care proxy in conjunction with the living will. The health care agent, in consultation with the attending physician, could likely reach opposite conclusions. The other approach is to be more specific in the living will, perhaps in the form of a general directive to consider all applicable circumstances.

However, the situation is not that simple. If the 85-year-old man devoutly believed that quality of life is not an issue for people to decide and that it is only up to God to determine when to take a life, he would want the same measures taken to preserve his life as would the younger woman. If that were his belief, the issues of what is heroic or not may be irrelevant. His living will should clarify these beliefs.

Step 6—Cease or withdraw heroic measures: If you meet the previous conditions and have determined not to have heroic measures, you should direct in your living will that all physicians and medical facilities, your family, and all those concerned with your care refrain from and cease extraordinary or heroic life-sustaining procedures and artificial maintenance and/or medical treatment.

Dignified Demise under Specified Conditions and with Specified Procedures

Some people feel that if their condition is so severe that recovery is not possible, a more affirmative plan should be taken to end their life. For many, perhaps most, such an approach may be close or equivalent to euthanasia (assisted suicide). If properly worded and planned so that the underlying disease or condition causes death, not the administration of drugs or the withdrawal of life support, courts might not view the cause of death as euthanasia.

If you have an incurable or irreversible severe mental or physical condition such that you are unable to interact meaningfully with the outside world or you are being kept alive by a respirator and are unable to move your limbs in any meaningful fashion, you may wish to direct that life support measures cease. To ensure that the condition is not misread and is in fact permanent, you might specify that the previously stated conditions continue for a minimum time period before such a determination is made. Some neurologists have stated that the continuation of such conditions for as little as two weeks provides adequate certainty. Others may disagree. You may wish to add a requirement that if the specified condition persists for at least 30 days, specified actions should be taken to cease medical support or even hasten death.

As in the story of the grandmother's farewell in the preceding chapter, you might request that friends and family be informed of your medical condition and be allowed, to the extent possible, to express their last wishes to you and, to the extent possible, for you to express your last wishes to them.

You may then request that you be placed on sufficient doses of morphine sulfate and/or other narcotics or sedatives, even if such measures shorten your life, to cease any physical or mental pain and so that you become unaware of the further steps. Once you are unaware, all heroic measures, including withdrawal of a respirator and feeding tube, can cease. All medical and surgical tests, treatments, and medications (other than the pain medications) can then be withheld or withdrawn, including but not restricted to diagnostic tests of any nature, artificially administered nutrition and hydration, antibiotics, artificial respirators, cardiac and pulmonary resuscitation, and surgical procedures of any nature.

A very few people might wish to go further and request that the process of their impending death be accelerated if they suffer from an incurable or irreversible severe physical condition and are in constant, unbearable pain. In these instances, they might direct any attending physician to speed their impending demise using whatever method is mutually determined appropriate or, if they are unable to communicate, such method as the attending physician, as to these wishes, deems appropriate provided such treatment is not illegal in the state where they reside. At the present time, this approach clearly exceeds the concept of the underlying illness causing the person's demise and passes into the realm of active euthanasia, something the law does not presently accept.

Perform All Procedures to Maintain Life

A living will does not have to indicate that you want "the plug pulled." In fact, if you want to request all medically appropriate procedures, you can and should do so. The media, the legal profession, and various right-to-die organizations have created dangerous misconceptions about the entire process. Too many people still believe that a living will is a statement that you don't want heroic health care measures taken when you are terminally ill. Your living will can be the opposite—a statement that you value life and wish every effort to be made to preserve your life. You can expressly direct that all medically appropriate measures be provided to sustain your life, regardless of your physical or mental condition and regardless of any hope for your recovering a normal life.

Myriad Other Options Exist

The choices are as varied as people making these decisions and the circumstances each person must confront. Whatever your starting point in preparing these key living will statements, tailor them, with the advice of your family, loved ones, medical adviser, social worker, religious adviser, and so on to meet your personal and specific wishes. If none of the previous clauses capture your feelings, modify them or prepare clauses that do represent your wishes.

Address Known Conditions

Most people haven't talked to their physicians about the impact of their current medical conditions on their end-of-life decisions. You should do so and specifically address them in your living will according the Margaret Galvin, Esq. of Holy

Name Hospital in Teaneck, New Jersey. For example, if you have a chronic respiratory condition such as emphysema or a chronic pulmonary condition and you state in your living will that you don't want to be put on a respirator, a situation might arise where putting you on a respirator for a temporary period may resolve the crises, but not impact your chronic condition. When the crisis is over, you might be able to resume a normal life (normal as defined subject to the chronic condition). If your family doesn't understand the distinction, they may question your being put on a respirator (or receiving other medical treatment to address your crises situation) and think your wishes (i.e., not to be put on a respirator) are not being carried out. If your living will stated that you are not to be put on a respirator if there is no hope of recovery, there may be no hope of recovery from the chronic condition of, for example, emphysema, but considerable hope of recovery from an immediate crisis. Improper wording can be a significant problem. Similarly, if someone with Alzheimer's doesn't address dementia in his or her living will, difficulties might arise as to what his or her wishes are. If you have early-stage Alzheimer's, help your family by addressing these issues while you still have capacity to do so.

NUTRITION AND HYDRATION

Nutrition and hydration (feeding and fluids) instructions can raise many issues. You should discuss these provisions in particular when you consult with your doctor to review living will decisions. How should *nutrition* and *hydration* be defined? When should, or should not, the provision of nutrition or hydration be considered heroic? Many people view nutrition and hydration as palliative, not medical in nature. From this perspective, it may never be appropriate to withdraw, or not provide, nutrition or hydration. After considering the following case study, you may still choose to conclude that nutrition and hydration may not be withheld or withdrawn, but you should do so with an understanding of what providing nutrition and hydration can entail.

Providing nutrition may require more than sitting you up in bed and feeding you. It might first begin with the insertion of a nasogastric tube, a tube threaded through your nose into your stomach through which liquid nutrition (such as Ensure) is injected. This tube can remain inserted for a week or two. Thereafter, if you still require artificial feeding, you will likely require a surgical procedure to insert a feeding tube into your stomach—a percutaneous endoscopic gastrostomy tube (PEG). In this case, you would be admitted to the hospital unit where these procedures are performed. You might have to be sedated with intravenous valium and/or a narcotic. A gastroenterologist inserts an endoscope through your mouth, down your esophagus (the tube between your throat and stomach), and into your stomach. The endoscope has a light on the end, which serves as the guide for a surgeon to make an incision through your skin and into your stomach. A tube is inserted and the gastroenterologist pulls it further into your body. The tube is secured in place with sutures (stitches). If this procedure is not appropriate for you given your condition, a more invasive approach to inserting a feeding tube can be done in the operating room. Whichever approach is used, once the tube is inserted, the outside end of the tube is then hooked up to liquid nutrition.

With this perspective, is providing nutrition and hydration really only palliative? Can you really state that it is not medical? If your 88-year-old aunt was terminally ill and demented, would you really want to put her through these procedures to add a few additional weeks to her life?

Case Study

A daughter watched her mother, a frail women in her late 80s, tragically deteriorate. The daughter ordered that a feeding tube be inserted on the basis of discussion with her religious adviser. Her mother suffered from acute dementia, heart failure, and kidney failure. The mother, as a result of her condition, kept pulling out her intravenous tubes through which she was receiving hydration. She had to be restrained with posey constraints (a constraint or tie used to bind a patient's wrists to a hospital bed to prevent movement). Having her wrists and ankles shackled to the bed was hardly a dignified or pleasant existence. Without insertion of the feeding tube, the mother might have survived for two to three weeks since she would not eat and was already frail. With the insertion of the feeding tube, the mother's traumatic last weeks were made even more invasive, disruptive, and painful. The benefit of the insertion of the PEG was that the patient lived for perhaps an additional week. That week was spent shrieking "Get me out of here!" and other incomprehensible statements. The family suffered terribly. The attending physician told the family at the time of the mother's admission that she would never be discharged. There was no hope. What was gained?

If religious concerns are important to you, how nutrition and hydration are addressed in your living will must be reviewed with your religious adviser because the removal of nutrition and hydration can have important implications to many religious beliefs. Many simply view the failure to provide nutrition or hydration, or their withdrawal, as no different from affirmatively starving a person: murder.

Because of the controversial nature of withdrawing nutrition and hydration, consider having a separate signature line next to any provision authorizing their withdrawal so no medical provider or court will have to question whether you really understood that you were authorizing the cessation of nutrition or hydration.

The following provisions indicate several optional approaches to addressing nutrition and hydration.

Never Withhold or Withdraw Nutrition or Hydration

If you believe that artificially administered nutrition and hydration should not be withheld, your living will should expressly state that they be administered whenever medically appropriate or even whenever medically feasible. If you believe that it is morally wrong to withhold nutrition and hydration, expressly state so in your living will.

Withhold Nutrition and Hydration Where Attending Physician Certifies

If any attending physician states in writing that you are, to a reasonable degree of medical certainty, in a terminal condition or a permanently unconscious state and that the provision (or continued provision) of nutrition and hydration will not, to a reasonable degree of medical certainty, prolong your life, provide comfort to you, or minimize your pain or discomfort, you may wish to authorize and direct the cessation of further nutrition or hydration.

Withhold Nutrition and Hydration Only in Accordance with the General Standards You've Set Governing Medical Care

Any artificially administered nutrition and hydration are considered by many as extraordinary and heroic measures and, as such, you may wish to provide that they can be withheld and withdrawn when other life-sustaining treatments are withheld or withdrawn in accordance with the general standards (e.g., quality of life, heroic measures) you've set forth in your living will.

Withhold Nutrition and Hydration If a Physician Certifies That There Is Loss of Cognition

If you are in a persistent vegetative state and there is no hope of recovery of brain function, you might still survive for decades. Is this really the quality of life you want? What about the burdens of your lingering on your family and loved ones? Many people prefer that nutrition and hydration be discontinued so that they might die a natural death, give closure to their loved ones, and maintain what they view as dignity in their last days. If this is how you feel, your living will should expressly authorize the cessation of nutrition and hydration if your attending physician can certify in writing that, to a reasonable degree of medical certainty, you have experienced a neurologically determined loss of cognition and communication from which you are unlikely to recover.

If this provision is contrary to applicable state law, you may request that your wishes be honored to the extent so permitted under state law. Alternatively, you should consider including in your living will a request that you be moved to another state that is more favorable to your wishes. This concept is discussed more fully in Chapter 5 on health care proxies because your health care agent is the person likely to exercise these powers on your behalf.

MEDICATION AND TREATMENTS TO ALLEVIATE PAIN AND SUFFERING

Pain relief is not a simple or obvious provision and, as such, was discussed in Chapter 2 as one of the major issues to address in your living will.

Provide Maximum Pain Relief

Whether procedures and treatments are to be withheld or withdrawn, you may wish that all palliative treatment and measures for your comfort and to alleviate your pain be continued. If this is your wish, your living will should expressly state so.

Should efforts to relieve your pain be continued even if such measures may shorten your life? What if pain relief may lead to permanent addiction? What if the pain relief may have potentially dangerous ancillary consequences, such as rendering you unconscious? What if the pain relief might lead to permanent physical damage?

Provide Pain Relief but Do Not Intentionally Hasten Death

A common concern among patients is that even though they want maximum pain relief, they do not want pain relief to cross the line of being used as a method to intentionally hasten the onset of death. It may be only a vague matter of degree. You might wish to state that pain relief should not affirmatively be used as a means of intentionally hastening your death. If you take this view, what, if any, meaningful pain relief might have this consequence?

PREGNANCY

Pregnancy raises a host of issues. Do you have the right to make decisions for your unborn fetus? What if you are unconscious and can no longer make decisions? Will decisions you have communicated earlier, such as in your living will, govern the treatment of your fetus when you are no longer able to? Several cases have held that you affirmatively have this right.

Another type of decision concerning pregnancy that you should consider addressing in your living will is the possibility that you are unable to make decisions. If a choice has to be made between a medical action to save you or your unborn fetus, what should be done? The best approach is to communicate your wishes while you are competent. This decision also has profound moral and religious implications.

One approach is to state, if it reflects your wishes, that preference be given to your life over the life of your fetus in any decisions that must be made. You might wish to further clarify the statement by adding that you should receive primary consideration over your fetus in any decision-making process.

Another approach is to state that all life-sustaining treatment be continued during the course of your pregnancy if there is reasonable hope of your child's being born healthy and able to lead a normal life and that your fetus receive primary consideration over you in any decision-making process. You might prefer this approach on the basis that you have at least had a life, albeit a shortened one, and your unborn fetus has not. Implicit in this statement is a concept of quality of life for your unborn fetus. This raises all the questions, uncertainties, and definition problems of your specifying a quality of life for yourself, as discussed previously.

Another option that may reflect your wishes is to state that no action be taken to favor your life or the life of your unborn fetus and that nature be allowed to take its course rather than medical professionals choosing one life over another.

WISHES CONCERNING LIVING ARRANGEMENTS

Your living will should address a broad range of issues, not just end-of-life medical decisions. One common issue that is very important to many people, especially elderly people who have seen both the good and the bad decisions friends have made concerning their residential care, is living arrangements. If you specify your wishes in the living will, there is a greater likelihood of those wishes being carried out.

You might wish to live your last days at home rather than in a hospital, nursing home, or other facility. You might, however, wish to remain at home only if such an arrangement would not jeopardize the chance of a meaningful recovery, impose undue burden on your family, or prevent your obtaining maximum pain relief for any illness. Alternatively, you might prefer that consideration be given to hospice and other palliative care if you have a terminal illness, rather than home care.

Although many people's initial reaction is to state that they want home care, reflect further as to whether you really wish this. Who will take care of you at home? If you are alone at home with a sole home health care worker, what type of care will you really receive? Who will monitor how you are treated? What type of interpersonal contact and stimulation will you receive? Will this really be better than being in a facility with activities and people?

WISHES CONCERNING KNOWLEDGE OF YOUR CONDITION

You might wish to specifically direct that all attending medical personnel fully and completely inform you of your medical conditions, including, but not limited to the fact that you may have a terminal illness and your anticipated life expectancy is compromised or shortened.

ORGAN DONATIONS

Organ donations should be discussed in some detail in your living will if you wish to be an organ donor. If you do not wish to be an organ donor, that decision should also be expressly stated. Should transplant of donated organs be limited to life-saving situations only? Should the potential donees be limited to family only? Should organ donations be limited to the sole purpose of transplant to save another person's life? Would you prefer to restrict organ donations to save a family member's life?

Can organ or tissue donations be used for more than mere transplant? If you wish to do so and have any religious affiliations, carefully consult with your religious adviser concerning organ donations for more than transplant to save lives. Some religious interpretations may restrict transplant to situations of preservation of life.

Should organ donations be permitted for medical study or educational purposes? If you wish to donate your body for medical study, you should contact a medical institution and make appropriate arrangements in advance.

Should any needed organs and tissues be donated? Do you prefer to limit donations to only certain organs and tissues?

An anatomical gift can be the ultimate act of kindness by giving life to another. In spite of the discomfort of addressing this issue, the needs are too great to ignore. In addition, many people falsely assume that religious restrictions prevent their being an organ donor.

If you wish to be an organ donor, you may be able to indicate your wishes on the back of your driver's license. Alternatively, especially if there are specific limitations on your wishes, you should consider signing an organ donor card to carry in your wallet. The decisions reflected on the card should be consistent with those indicated in your living will.

FUNERAL, CREMATION, AND RELATED ARRANGEMENTS

Importance of Addressing Funeral Service, Burial, and Related Matters

Don't assume that your family or loved ones will know what type of funeral, burial, or other arrangements you want. Even if they do know, it's often best to set forth some decisions in your living will to avoid the issues of different views among survivors. The fact that your loved ones all seem amicable now may not be the reality following your demise. Too often, in the emotional upheaval following the death of a parent or other family member, friction, feuds, and other issues that had simmered below the surface break out with a fury. Decide now whether you should be buried next to your first, second, or third spouse. Don't assume that even religious rituals are obvious to your surviving loved ones. There is much variation in not only levels of religious observance among different family members but also religions.

Religious Principles That Should Govern Funeral and Other Arrangements

Many people, even those who choose not to have religious restrictions apply to the determinations of whether life support should be continued, wish to have funeral or burial rituals to conform with their religious background. If you are undecided, consider that surviving loved ones often find solace in religious rituals and customs.

If you wish cremation and interment of your remains, you should indicate this, along with any preferences for where and how your remains should be interred.

You might wish to specify that your funeral service, arrangements, and burial be in accordance with a particular religion's customs. If so, consider whether there are options within that set of customs that you need to address.

Example: If you are Catholic, you might specify that you wish to receive last rites and that your funeral service be in accordance with Catholic religious customs.

There are a number of related decisions you might wish to address in other estate planning documents. In your health care proxy, you might wish to authorize your agent to purchase a burial plot and marker and to make such other related arrangements if you have not already done so. If you have a request that might create some costs, such as a burial in a foreign country, purchase of a mausoleum, and so on, discuss with your attorney inclusion of the request in your will. Your executor will then be able to pay for these costs and finances will not be an issue.

NO TIME LIMIT; DURATION

You may want to specify that you wish to limit the effectiveness of your living will to a fixed time period or until a specified date. If you don't specify a limit (in most cases, you probably would not wish to do so), your living will should state that it will remain in full force and effect for as long as you are alive. Some institutions or medical care providers may be reluctant to rely on a living will out of concern that you may have modified or revoked it. This issue can be addressed by stating in your living will that any person or institution that relies on it will not be held responsible if it had been revoked previously unless that person or institution had received written notice of revocation or change.

MISCELLANEOUS LIVING WILL PROVISIONS

There are a host of miscellaneous provisions that you might wish to include in your living will. Some may tailor your living will to your specific issues. Others may address issues of state law because the rules can differ so substantially from state to state; thus, it is important to have an attorney in your state re-view and supervise the signing of your living will (and health care proxy).

Morally Binding

Because of the vagaries of state law and the changes and de-velopments in the laws affecting living wills, you might wish to include a general direction stating that if, for any reason, your living will is not valid or a wish you request is not legally valid, you expect your family, physicians, and all those concerned with your care to act as if morally bound to act in accordance with your living will directions. To encourage compliance, you might also wish to state that anyone following your wishes should be free from any liability and responsibility for having done so (indemnification).

Revocation and Cancellation of Prior Living Wills

If you've signed prior living wills, you will likely want the most current living will to superseded any prior ones. This is important to avoid any conflicts if the provisions between them are different. To accomplish this, your living will can state that it revokes any prior living will, health care power of attorney, or health care proxy executed by you.

Copies of Document

It is difficult to ensure that anyone who needs your living will can have an original. Although many health care providers will readily accept a photocopy, to facilitate the use of copies, your living will should state that a copy is as valid as an original.

Severability

Your living will should state that its provisions are severable so that the invalidity of one or more provisions will not affect any other provisions. Thus, if one of the wishes you've stated violates state law, the entire document won't be invalidated. This is important in light of the dynamic nature of the laws applying to living wills. It is especially important if you have unusual health care wishes.

Competency to Execute Document

For your living will to be valid, you have to be competent. Although admittedly self-serving, your living will should state that you understand its full import and that you are emotionally and mentally competent to execute it.

Construction and Interpretation of This Document

Should legislation or regulations be enacted after the execution of your living will, you want your living will, to the extent necessary to make it valid and enforceable, to be interpreted so it complies with such future legislation or regulations in the manner that most closely approximates the wishes you've indicated.

Most legal documents specify that the laws of a particular state should govern the document. Your living will should similarly specify that it is executed in a particular state and should be interpreted in accordance with a particular state's laws. You might, however, become ill in another state, whose laws may differ from the laws of the state you declared should govern your living will. If this occurs, that other state might provide that the laws of the state governing the living will apply. All this complexity and uncertainty should concern you and motivate you to be cautious. To the extent feasible, your living will should be prepared and signed in a manner that is likely to be accepted in as many states as possible. For example, although the state in which you sign your living will may provide that the document is valid with merely one witness, you should consider having two witnesses and a notary so that your living will is more likely to be accepted in other states. Often, living wills (and health care proxies) are drafted to meet the specific requirements of one state. However, if there is no significant cost or difficulty in meeting a higher standard, you should opt for the higher standard.

SIGNING YOUR LIVING WILL

You should sign your living will, if feasible, in the presence and under the supervision of an attorney in your state and before two witnesses and a notary. The witnesses should be acquainted with you and believe you are of sound mind and under no constraint, duress, or undue influence. The witnesses should not be related to you by blood or marriage and should not be entitled to any portion of your estate in the event of your death. If they were, there could be an ulterior motive that makes their witnessing your living will questionable. The witnesses should not be physicians attending to you as a patient. The witnesses should be over 18 years of age.

QUESTIONS TO CONSIDER

1. What medical efforts do you want to be made on your behalf? Under what conditions? Heroic measures? Nutrition and/or hydration? Pain relief?
2. Are there any particular personal issues that you want addressed in your living will?
3. Do quality-of-life decisions affect your decision making? How do you define quality of life?
4. What about funeral and burial arrangements? Have you considered what will be best for your survivors?
5. Have the miscellaneous legal formality provisions discussed in this chapter been included in the living will form you signed?

CHAPTER SUMMARY

Signing a simple living will, without carefully considering the many personal, medical, and legal issues involved, is unlikely to address your concerns and needs. To ensure that your wishes are carried out, the issues in this chapter should be considered, evaluated, discussed with loved ones and advisers, and then implemented.

4 RELIGIOUS ISSUES AND LIVING WILLS

RELIGIOUS PREFERENCES OR LACK OF RELIGIOUS PREFERENCES SHOULD BE SPECIFIED

Religious considerations are vitally important to every living will. Do not assume that because you are not religious you can ignore religious implications. Your family, loved ones, or others may have religious beliefs that conflict with your health care wishes, or they may not be certain about your beliefs. Therefore, whether you do or do not wish your end-of-life decisions to be based on religious beliefs, you need to communicate those decisions.

If you have strong religious convictions, it is imperative to specifically address religious concerns to avoid having your beliefs compromised if you are unable to express your desires. Since health care wishes are such a personal matter, it is also vital to address religious concerns so that your family members or others involved with your health care do not push their beliefs (or lack of beliefs) on you.

The legal community, right-to-die organizations, and many others involved with the health care decision process have all but ignored religious considerations. Many, perhaps most, people signing living wills while they are healthy aren't concerned about religious issues. Many of these same people, when faced with a major catastrophe such as terminal illness or loss of a close family member, fall back to their religious roots for guidance and comfort. Unfortunately, it may then be too late for these people, or their loved ones, to remedy the situation. The solution is to give consideration to the religious implications of the entire health care process while you are able to so that if you or your family experience tragedy, you won't have to regret what was done.

Regardless of religious convictions, your living will should communicate your decision. If you were born to parents with a particular religious affiliation, other members of your family might assume it appropriate to consult with clergy of your religious background before making a decision. This might, or might not, be your wish. Religiously influenced decisions could differ from the types of decisions you might prefer. For example, several religions restrict the ability to cease heroic measures as most people would define the term. If you want nutrition and hydration withdrawn when there is no hope of your regaining quality of life, it is important to communicate whether you wish religious principles to be considered in making this decision.

Religious doctrines may have a very specific effect on what can be done medically to sustain or not sustain life. Regardless of how you presently feel about the effects the tenets of your faith may have on these decisions, it can be a terrible mistake not to address these issues with your clergy. Your family's religious convictions should be considered. It may be possible to carry out your wishes with perhaps only modifications and yet be within the religious tenets of your faith.

If you decide, after consulting with your clergy and discussions with your family, that you wish to take a position contrary to the tenets of your faith, your living will should indicate this in very precise terms. You may wish to provide the name and address of a clergy member to be consulted for interpretations of your religious beliefs and the name of a religious organization or institution to be contacted should the clergy member not be available.

The remainder of this chapter addresses religious considerations of many different religious groups. These comments and sample clauses are based on experiences with clients over many years. Not all religions have been addressed, and for religions that are addressed, not all components of that faith have been addressed. It is important that you discuss the form and position you wish to keep with your personal religious adviser. Thus, the following should be viewed as no more than a starting point to open a dialogue.

HOSPITAL INQUIRIES AS TO RELIGIOUS PREFERENCES

The uncertainty of religious affiliation might be resolved in that most hospitals record religious affiliation on the hospital chart and computer system on admission. "This information could be relied on," suggests Margaret Galvin of Holy Name Hospital, Teaneck, New Jersey. If the existence of a living will is noted in the system, on subsequent visits, patients are asked whether they have amended their living will. A mere indication of religious affiliation, however, may not afford the opportunity to provide the depth of clarity given the wide range of religious observances even within the same religion.

LIVING WILL PROVISIONS TO ADDRESS RELIGIOUS CONVICTIONS

Regardless of the religious beliefs you may apply to your living will, there are a number of points to consider. First, should the religious beliefs specified apply to all aspects of your living will or only certain components? The two most common approaches are to have religious beliefs govern all aspects of your living will or to have religious beliefs apply only to funeral service and burial. The latter approach is common because many people wish to be respectful of the faith but are concerned that religious restrictions will force them to be maintained on life support long after they have no hope of recovery or quality of life. Although religious restrictions can prevent the withdrawal of life support in some situations, religious restrictions are often more flexible, sensitive, and sophisticated than many people realize. Before concluding that your personal wishes won't be met because of religious restrictions, consult with your religious adviser.

If you do condition any portion or all of your living will and end-of-life decisions on religious beliefs, it might be helpful to designate a particular religious adviser (and successor) or an organization to advise on and resolve any issues. If your agent under your health care proxy is reasonably knowledgeable of your religious beliefs, you might suggest that a religious adviser be selected in your agent's reasonable discretion and in accordance with your statement of religious beliefs.

If you do designate a religious adviser, your living will should state that no health care provider should be required in any situation to get approval from such religious adviser in order to carry out your instructions. This statement is recommended so that health care providers would not insist that your religious adviser, in addition to your agent, sign off on a medical decision, which could create administrative difficulties in your living will.

BUDDHIST CONSIDERATIONS IN ESTATE PLANNING

How would a Buddhist orientation affect the tenor of a living will and health care proxy? There are significant differences between how the Buddhist philosophy and how most Western religions view death, and these differing concepts should be conveyed in the drafting of a living will. No Buddhist would want to suffer unnecessary pain, so provisions authorizing and directing pain relief would be appropriate.

However, Buddhists also wish to die consciously. Your state of consciousness at the moment of death is believed to strongly influence your rebirth in the next life. As a result, it is important that your living will convey your desire for consciousness, since this perspective can differ considerably from the way many Westerners view the process.

Buddhist traditions are not necessarily consistent among adherents, so standardized forms or language to address all Buddhists are not feasible. Some background on the development of Buddhism is provided to illustrate some of the many differences and diversities. Unlike many other religions, Buddhism developed and spread to many different countries and, over the centuries, has adopted many diverse local customs that are not inconsistent with the original Buddhist philosophy and approach to life. As a result, a Buddhist with origins in Taiwan might have a number of customs distinct from those of a Buddhist whose origins are Japan or elsewhere. Thus, many of the comments, while applicable to a broad range of Buddhists, can be subject to substantial local or customary differences. Being alert to this diversity is important to ensure that a Buddhist practitioner's wishes are addressed.

Removal of Body

Many living wills mention a preference for a particular type of funeral, cremation, service, and so on. What practices and customs do Buddhist beliefs suggest, and what might Buddhist practitioners wish to consider mentioning in their living wills? In substantial contrast to many other religious faiths, the Buddhist custom is to avoid removing the body from the place of death for at least seven days. A number of rituals or customs are performed following death. The belief is that the spirit of the deceased can remain with the body until rebirth, which occurs within seven days, so the body should not be moved or tampered with during this seven-day period. Because of the impossibility of adhering to these customs in a hospital, it is strongly recommended that a Buddhist practitioner endeavor to spend his or her last days at home, where the ability to respect such traditions would be more likely. Thus, a living will or letter of instruction for a Buddhist should suggest that, if feasible, he or she be permitted to spend the last days in an appropriate facility or home.

Following death and after the minimum one-week waiting period, either cremation or burial is permissible. Buddhism itself does not require either cremation or burial; the decision is usually culturally based. Thus, a Buddhist might wish to specify in the living will the type of funeral service preferred. In addition to the cultural differences that dictate either cremation or burial, there are many cultural differences for the type of funeral service. Although there are common elements among the different Asian traditions—in particular, the practice of reading from the Buddhist holy books, the *Sutras*—there are many factors that vary from culture to culture.

Other Buddhist Traditions

It is common during the last living days or hours of a Buddhist for loved ones to read from the *Sutras* and to converse with the dying person, because it is believed that even if a patient is unconscious and incapable of communication, hearing might remain. It is a Buddhist belief that hearing is the last sense to go.

Other traditions and customs exist for Buddhists before death, including having a statue or picture of the Holy Buddha or a bodhisattva and a book of the holy *Sutras* in the patient's room soon before his or her death. A very important custom is that of burning incense, a symbol of the Buddhist path; the smoke rises upward just as thoughts should be of a spiritual tenor. The slow and consistent burning of incense is a sign of spiritual growth and is symbolic of the slow and consistent path that is necessary over the course of a lifetime to attain enlightenment. The burning of incense in particular raises considerable difficulties in any medical institution. Many hospitals have tried to look the other way for perhaps the burning of a single stick of incense. Thus, the preference is for the patient to spend his or her last days at home so these customs can be followed. The general objective is to pursue as natural a death as possible from the Buddhist perspective.

Do Not Resuscitate Orders

From the Buddhist standpoint, if the patient has severe brain damage, you would not want to resuscitate the patient. Rather, the patient should be allowed to pass on. The goal is to die with as clear and calm a mind as possible. Thus, the heroic measures that might otherwise be taken could be contrary to a major lifetime objective of a Buddhist patient. Because of the many differences in Buddhist traditions from those of most Western religions, it is strongly advisable that Buddhists carry a wallet card indicating that they are of the Buddhist tradition, perhaps even summarizing some of its key points.

Organ Donations

The difficulty with organ donations under Buddhist tradition is that the body is not to be disturbed for seven days. On the other hand, Buddhism views any selfless act of charity to help another as very admirable. Thus, there is a tremendous incentive to try to assist others in need. There are differences among the cultures in how a Buddhist from any given tradition views the concept of organ donations in light of this conflict. Those of Chinese descent often, out of their great respect for ancestry, have a tremendous reluctance to permit organ donations of a deceased family member. On the other hand, Tibetan Buddhists believe that a dead person no longer resides in the body; thus, organ donations are more acceptable to Tibetans.

HINDUISM AND ESTATE PLANNING

Hindus believe in reincarnation—all life forms, including humans, go through a recurring cycle of birth, death, and rebirth. The consequences of a person's actions in his or her lifetime determine the form and fate of reincarnation. The Four Yogas, or disciplines, may be followed by all Hindus. The Four Yogas—Jnana Yoga (yoga of knowledge), Karma Yoga (yoga of work),

Bhakti Yoga (yoga of devotion), and Saranagati Yoga (yoga of absolute surrender to God)—form the four paths to discerning the true nature of reality, enlightenment, and self-realization.

Living wills and health care issues are important but raise concern to many faiths. In executing a living will, a Hindu faces many issues.

Life Support

Life support is not permitted. Hindus believe a person lives as long as he or she naturally can and accepts the end as and when it happens. If a person has suffered severe brain damage and there is no hope of recovery, there is no basis for prolonging life by artificial means. Do not resuscitate (DNR) orders should be standard for every Hindu. If a bad drug or reaction to a drug were the cause of this issue, DNR would still apply. A medical mistake would not be considered acceptable as that person's destiny. Supporting a life by artificial means is not permitted spiritually. A Hindu may not be kept on a respirator because it interferes with the life cycle. Blood transfusion and dialysis are very difficult and personal issues and should be carefully discussed with the persons involved. Taking medication and health care is permitted, but supporting life artificially is not.

Pain Relief

Pain relief is an important issue to address. Beliefs can differ considerably from those assumed to be natural by many Western faiths. For instance, if a Hindu were dying in an unconscious state, it is not viewed essential to maintain life through heroic measures. With the cycle of birth and rebirth, deferring death when there is no consciousness is not as critical as from a Western perspective. However, trying to maintain consciousness at the time of death is an important goal for a Hindu. A Hindu wants to be conscious so that certain important rituals and chants can be performed before and at the time of death.

Pregnancy and Euthanasia

The life of a mother or the fetus cannot be taken to save one or the other. Euthanasia is not permitted. To the Hindu, suicide, euthanasia, and abortion are no different from murder. An elderly person who is suffering and who is given medication to hasten death is considered murdered. Mercy killing is not permitted.

Other Hindu Considerations

According to Hindu tradition, it is not proper to die in a bed. If death is expected within a few hours, the person should be laid out on the floor and an oil lamp lit by his or her head. The family should try to give the person holy water and chant prayers for the peaceful passing of the soul. The person's lying on the floor represents the inevitability of death and the futility of materialistic affluence. These customs cannot always be implemented because family members sometimes prefer to keep the person in a health care facility to try to prolong life. These customs are difficult to perform in a typical hospital setting, and that encourages a Hindu to spend his or her last days at home.

According to Hindu law, the body should be cremated within 24 hours of death. However, a female child before marriage should be buried and a male child before baptism, which occurs generally at age 8, should be buried and not cremated. These ancient rules are not followed by all Hindus, and the living will should be specific. Funeral rites are always performed by the oldest male child. If a person does not have a son, it is customary to name a male family member to perform the rites.

The mourning or quarantine period is for 10 days after death, including the day of death. On the 11th, 12th, and 13th days, various funeral rites are to be performed for the departed soul to rest in peace, and donations and charitable gifts are made.

For the first year after death, every month, on the day the person died, special rituals are performed by the sons. After one year, on the anniversary day of death, prayers are offered by the sons for the rest of their lives. Feeding the poor and charitable giving are important parts of these rituals.

After cremation, the ashes should be immersed in a holy river, specifically, the holy river Ganges in India. A will should specify if the ashes should be taken to India. The ashes should be maintained in a safe and dignified manner until someone returns to India to deliver them.

Hindus believe in reincarnation. Human life is a transition point. The results of a person's actions are reflected in his or her next life. Through actions, a person can elevate himself or herself to the level of angels or decline to the level of animals. Humans have a highly developed consciousness to attain salvation, which is freedom from the cycle of repeated births and deaths. Animals and plants do not have this advanced consciousness. Positive actions will be weighed against negative actions, and the ultimate salvation may take thousands of births and rebirths to achieve. Provisions in a Hindu will could address this issue.

The goal of Hindu philosophy is to guide a person for spiritual elevation, not material success. The path of desire, or the attractions of worldly success, is ephemeral and seductive. The spiritual way has sanctions for material advancement, but should not take the dominant role.

JEWISH ISSUES IN ESTATE AND FINANCIAL PLANNING

When evaluating Jewish issues affecting living wills, differences exist among different branches of Judaism. The following discussion addresses primarily Orthodox views; therefore, different considerations might apply to adherents of different branches of Judaism. While a rabbi can assist doctors and family in reaching a decision that is in accordance with Jewish law and a person's religious beliefs, an awareness of the person's feelings can be important in properly guiding the family and physicians.

Numerous issues in the living will and health care proxy are affected by Jewish religious doctrines. The following discussion presents some issues that should be discussed with a rabbi and addressed to the extent desired in the living will.

There are a host of matters to be addressed concerning religious issues and living wills. For additional information about issues or concerns you might have, contact: Agudath Israel of America, 84 William Street, New York, NY 10038; Union for Traditional Judaism, 261 East Lincoln Avenue, Mount Vernon, NY 10552; or Rabbinical Council of America, 275 Seventh Avenue, New York, NY 10001.

Life Is Sacred

Life is sacred. The fact that the quality of life can never be what you would hope for cannot alone justify a decision to shorten life. Life is sacred, even when it can be for only a limited period of time. So great is the value of life that, in some instances, a patient can, according to Jewish law, be encouraged, convinced, or even forced to accept medical treatment. Everything must generally be done to save and prolong life (*pikuach nefesh*). However, Jewish law does not require that every life-saving measure be taken in every situation.

Even a terminal, near-death patient (*goses*) is considered in all respects to be a living person. To hasten the death of such a person, even with minor steps such as closing his or her eyes, can be equated with murder.

It can, however, be permissible to passively remove a mere impediment to death since it is improper to prolong the act of dying. For example, where a patient experiences great pain and suffering, medications that will merely prolong a life of suffering may be refused. It is even permissible to pray for someone in great pain to die to end the suffering.

The application of the distinction between these standards, however, must be applied on a case-by-case basis.

Aggressive versus Passive Action

The intent behind a medical decision can be important. If a doctor recommends surgery to save a patient's life, not to undertake the surgery would be tantamount to an active decision to die—called a *Kum va' Asseh* (stand and do), an active or aggressive position. Jewish law would require surgery. Where the surgery itself could entail a risk to life, Jewish law might not require surgery. The decision in this instance would be called a *shev v'al ta'asseh* (sit and don't do), a passive decision. Where the risk to life of a procedure is greater then the risk of not performing the procedure, nonintervention can be chosen. These principles can be applied in various situations. Where a decision concerning resuscitation must be made, if the patient's general health is so frail that resuscitation itself could entail substantial risks to life, resuscitation may be avoided under the principle of *shev v'al ta'asseh*.

These principles can create important differences in Jewish law between withholding treatment and withdrawing treatment.

Definition of Death

The issue of when death is deemed to occur has profound religious implications and repercussions to several health care decisions. Some rabbis have addressed the position that death should be defined as brainstem death. Other rabbinic authorities interpret Jewish law as providing for a definition of death based on the historical definition of cessation of cardiac and respiratory function.

Administration of Pain Relief

Pain relief, where the intent is to make the patient more comfortable, but not to hasten death, is permitted, even where the administration of pain relief can hasten death.

Respirators

If a patient is on a respirator that is assisting breathing, disconnecting the respirator is generally prohibited. If a respirator may be disconnected temporarily to care for the patient or maintain the equipment, the question of whether it must be reconnected can be difficult. If a respirator is merely artificially maintaining breathing, the response may differ. However, if the patient has died (see previous definition of death under Jewish law), removal is mandatory because not to do so would merely delay burial, which is not permitted.

Nutrition and Hydration

The refusal of food and water is generally not permitted. Jewish law, according to some authorities, views the provision of food and water as a supportive care that must be given, and not as a medical treatment that can be avoided. However, where inserting a tube, such as a gastric tube, is inherently harmful, there may be a basis to argue against insertion. The side effects of the tube feeding must be evaluated before a decision is made not to insert such tubes. The evaluation of the medical risks and the implications of such risks to Jewish law are dependent on the specific circumstances of each patient. The issue is a difficult one, since the failure to provide nutrition and hydration will certainly and directly lead to death. Thus, great care must be exercised in making any general statements concerning withdrawal or nonprovision of nutrition and hydration.

Life Support and Heroic Measures

Life support and heroic measures often cannot be withdrawn if the result is to hasten the onset of death. This is possibly akin to murder. However, the view from Orthodox, Conservative, Reform, and Reconstructionist branches can vary. A rabbi should be consulted in modifying the sample provisions concerning heroic measures. The fact that the quality of life cannot be what you hope for cannot justify a decision to shorten life. Life is sacred, and everything possible must generally be done to save and to prolong life, even for one extra second (*pikuach nefesh*).

Do Not Resuscitate (DNR) Orders

Cardiopulmonary resuscitation can be effective in many patients; therefore, a blanket DNR order often violates Jewish law. However, where the patient's health is so frail that the procedure would be medically futile or severe injuries might result from the process, refusal of resuscitation may be sanctioned.

Surgical Procedures

The determination of whether surgical procedures can be denied must be made with consideration of many of the principles discussed previously. If there is no significant chance for cure, surgery that also has substantial inherent risks may be declined. Rabbi Moshe Feinstein stated that where the chances of a successful surgery are about 50 percent, it may be undertaken. Where the chances are greater than 50 percent, it must be undertaken.

Autopsies

Autopsies and dissections are, absent extenuating circumstances, generally prohibited by Jewish law unless the autopsy can be shown necessary to save another's life.

Organ Donation

The perception among most Jews is that organ donation is improper and that every limb is to be buried with the deceased. This perception is just not correct. Organ donations present an unusual opportunity to save another's life. This, however, is a radical change in Jewish thinking and requires that both traditional psychology and the traditional interpretations of *Halacha*, Jewish law, be considered.

Organs cannot be harvested until the patient has died as defined under Jewish law. There is a question as to the definition of death. Where a definition of brainstem death (*hutaz rosho*—the head was severed) is considered the controlling definition of death, certain organs, such as the heart, may be removed for the purpose of saving another life. Where a cardiopulmonary definition of death is used, the question of donation of certain organs becomes more problematic.

In addition, for any organ donation to be permitted, it must be predicated on the principle of saving a life. Therefore, organ donation can be permitted only where the organs are used to save a life and not to have the organs placed in a donor pool. Donations of corneas to an eye bank are considered acceptable because of the frequent use. Consider including the following sample clause in the living will:

Sample Clause: The saving of a life takes precedence over all but three Jewish legal (*Halachic*) imperatives: murder, idolatry, and adultery. Accordingly, no barriers exist to donation of my organs once I am deceased if they are obtained in accordance with *Halachic* requirements. These requirements include maintaining the highest standards of respect for human dignity. Vital organs such as my heart and liver may be donated after I have been declared dead by a competent neurologist based on clinical and/or radiological evidence. For these purposes, death shall be defined as brainstem death together with other accepted neurological criteria. Since organs can be life saving, mine may be donated, and I urge my family to do so.

Burial

Jewish law has a number of requirements concerning burial. To ensure that burial is in accordance with Jewish law, advance arrangements with a Jewish burial society, a Chevra Kadisha, should be considered. The family and health care agent should be notified of arrangements.

Pregnancy

Where the fetus threatens the life of the mother and where the fetus is not considered born (as *born* is defined by Jewish law), the mother's life must be preserved, even at the expense of the life of the fetus (*rodaif*). Once the fetus is born, this principle would no longer apply.

Specifying a Rabbi

Given the complexity of the many religious issues, one approach that most religious experts tend to accept is to use a living will form that states that the client wants Jewish religious principals to apply and that a particular rabbi should be contacted to resolve any questions (refer to the religious convictions section of the sample living will to name a particular rabbi). If the particular rabbi is not available, a named organization should be consulted.

CATHOLIC RELIGIOUS ISSUES AND ESTATE PLANNING

Living wills raise a host of Catholic religious issues, the following of which are but a few. It is advisable for a Catholic to sign a living will clarifying that Catholic religious observances should be respected. The living will puts the person in control of decision making when he or she cannot be in physical control. It is also of great help to the family, which is always torn at such difficult times.

Unfortunately, many Catholics assume the Church mandates that they be kept alive no matter what. As a result, many don't sign living wills in accordance with Catholic religious principles. But this is an unfortunate misunderstanding. Catholics can secure living wills that are consistent with not only their personal wishes, but also their religious heritage.

Optional clauses can be added to a standard living will to conform it to individual Catholic ideals. These clauses should be integrated into the body of the standard living will (Chapter 3) in addition to or instead of some of the standard clauses. Be certain to consult a priest to confirm any provisions. You may wish to contact the Archdiocese of Newark, 31 Mulberry Street, Newark, NJ 07102 (973) 497-4253 or the New Jersey Catholic Conference, 211 N. Warren Street, Trenton, NJ (609) 599-2110, for additional information.

The following examples of general clauses are meant to infuse the living will with a sense of the Catholic tenets. These particular clauses, if added, should be integrated into the Recitals component of the standard living will (Introductory clauses):

Sample Clauses: WHEREFORE, God is the creator and preserver of life. Since life is a journey from God and back to God, with death as part of that journey, it follows that life is sacred, but not an ultimate value. From this perspective, death is not a failure or an absolute evil, but the culmination of the journey.

WHEREFORE, my Christian heritage holds that life is the gift of a loving God. I see life as a sacred trust over which I can claim stewardship, but not ownership. Therefore, I believe that euthanasia and suicide constitute an unwarranted destruction of human life and are not morally permissible. I understand, as a Catholic, that I may never choose to cause my death as an end or a means.

Heroic Measures

The Church does not mandate that a person be kept alive no matter what. The Church believes that a person can decide to avoid overly invasive and experimental procedures, not ordinary means of care. "Ordinary means" could include feeding someone, ensuring that he or she has air to breathe, and so on. The Church believes that a patient must continue to receive ordinary care; otherwise, you are effectively acting to cause the patient's death. The extraordinary means go beyond this and seek to reverse a process that is already underway. Extraordinary means can be refused, but not ordinary means.

The following is a "no heroic measures" directive, as it is understood based on various interpretations of the Catholic church. It can be added to or substituted for the general no heroic measures directive found in a typical living will to conform a living will to include the Catholic beliefs deemed important.

No Heroic Measures Language as Understood by the Catholic Church Shall Be Taken

---

Sample Language: If I (1) have an incurable or irreversible, severe mental or severe physical condition; (2) am in a state of permanent unconsciousness or profound dementia; (3) am severely injured, and in any of these cases there is no reasonable expectation of recovering from such severe, permanent condition and regaining any meaningful quality of life, then in any such event, it is my desire and intent that heroic life-sustaining procedures and extraordinary maintenance or medical treatment, as understood in the moral tradition of the Catholic church, be withheld and withdrawn.

It is not my desire to prolong my life through mechanical means where my body is no longer able to perform vital bodily functions on its own and where there is little likelihood of ever regaining any meaningful quality of life. The condition and degree of severity and permanence contemplated by this provision are of such a nature and degree of permanent illness, injury, disability, or accompanied by pain such that the average Catholic person might contemplate, in the moral tradition of the Catholic church, the decisions addressed herein (whether such person would make the decisions I have made herein).

In any such event, I direct all physicians and medical facilities in whose care I may be and my family and all those concerned with my care to refrain from and cease extraordinary or heroic life-sustaining procedures and artificial maintenance and/or medical treatment, as understood in the moral tradition of the Catholic church. The procedures and treatment to be withheld and withdrawn include, without limitation, surgery, antibiotics, cardiac and pulmonary resuscitation, ventilation, or other respiratory support.

Nutrition and Hydration

Withholding nutrition and hydration for a Catholic should be done only if in accordance with Catholic religious doctrines. Generally, nutrition and hydration are considered ordinary means and should not be withheld. To withhold nutrition or hydration could be equivalent to starving a person to death. Attorneys must exercise care in using standard living will forms because many authorize withholding nutrition and hydration, contrary to the wishes of many Catholic clients.

The following is an example of a clause that could be included in the nutrition and hydration section of the living will to conform the will to Catholic tenets:

Sample Clause: Withhold nutrition and hydration only if permissible under Catholic religious doctrines. Any artificially administered nutrition and hydration (feeding and fluids), if considered extraordinary and heroic measures in accordance with standards and principles as set forth by the Catholic church, may be withheld or withdrawn. For purposes of this provision, nutrition and hydration shall include, by way of example and not limitation, tube feedings, Corpak tubes, nasogastric tubes, Levin tubes, gastrostomy tube, or hyperalimentation.

Pain Relief

Where the objective is to relieve pain, any action is always proper. If the objective is to actively hasten the onset of death, it is inappropriate to authorize such an action in the Church's view. God is the lord and master of life; we are not. The Church believes that we are always safe in God's hands because He loves us more than we love ourselves. Therefore, to actively hasten death would be a violation of these fundamental beliefs.

An example of a possible directive to be integrated into the living will to address the issue of pain relief is:

Sample Clause: Provide pain relief to the extent permissible under Catholic religious doctrine. Where procedures and treatment are to be withheld or withdrawn, I wish that all treatment and measures for my comfort, and to alleviate my pain, be continued, so long as they do not actively hasten the onset of death.

Pregnancy

Catholic women should consider Catholic religious issues concerning pregnancy in their living wills. If there is a physical condition in the mother that should be corrected, and if the fetus, incidentally and by accident, dies, that is permissible. But no affirmative action that would likely cause the death of the fetus can be taken. You cannot choose the life of the mother over the life of the fetus. All life is sacred and is in God's hands. This is important to address because it can differ from what many people might assume if uninformed.

The following clause is an example of a possible directive concerning pregnancy. It should be integrated into the pregnancy provision of the living will to address Catholic doctrine about pregnancy and end-of-life situations:

Sample Clause: Issues of pregnancy should be resolved in accordance with Catholic religious doctrine. My life shall not have precedence over the life of my fetus if a choice must be made between my survival and the survival of my fetus. My fetus's life shall not have precedence over my life if a choice must be made between my survival and the survival of my fetus. I direct that no action be taken which would likely lead to the death of either myself or my fetus, even if such action is necessary to save either myself or my fetus.

Organ Donation and the Definition of Death

The Catholic church's definition of death mirrors that of many state statutes. Death is the irreversible cessation of all brain functions. This definition facilitates the possibility of organ donations. The Church is not in favor nor does it oppose organ donations. It leaves the decision up to the individual to do what his or her heart desires. There is no right or wrong in the eyes of the Church when it comes to organ donations. It is enough to have a simple directive stating, for example: "I am (not) willing to donate any organs that may help others."

Last Rites

Last rites are an important ritual for those facing death. They include the sacrament of the anointing of the sick, confession, and reception of communion. The presumption is that any Catholic would want last rites. However, given the diversity of today's society and to avoid any confusion, the living will should specify that last rites should be given.

Funeral Provisions

Too often, Catholics dispense with a religious service and use a funeral chapel's service instead. The service at the parish church for a funeral mass, which is very important, is thus missed. This service is important for the deceased, who, Catholics believe, can gain from the prayers of the congregation and the grace of the sacramental action. It is also a tremendous consolation for the family and friends. When the bereaved pray together, they can experience their own grace-filled strength and the support of the others who pray with them—important for the solace of the survivors. For Catholics, the Mass in church is the appropriate way to say farewell to a loved one. Catholics should consider including an express request for such a service in their living will; even if personally indifferent, for the benefit of the survivors, it should still be addressed.

Cremation is allowed, although not necessarily preferred.

ISLAMIC CONSIDERATIONS

Three sources are relevant to determining Islamic law that affects living wills. Every Muslim is under the obligation to follow the Koran. There are also sayings of the Prophet Mohammad, which were made relating to these matters based on Koranic injunctions. Finally, there are decisions called *Fiqh*, which is analogous to case law in the American legal system. These *Fiqhs* are analyses by jurists of the issues covered by the Koran and the sayings of the Prophet. If these sources are silent, a decision must be made that is consistent with the spirit of them.

Islamic Law and Living Wills

Islamic law permits the use of living wills. Decisions concerning health are primarily given to the physicians. Procedures that will enable someone to be restored to health should be done. If a medical procedure would merely keep a person alive but would not restore the person to health, it need not be done. If the only result is to artificially keep someone alive on life support, the procedure is not mandatory under Islamic law, but heroic measures may be continued if the family so wishes. Generally, these decisions should be made by the physician.

Issues for every Muslim to consider include the definition of death, organ donations, and the appointment of an attorney or agent on his or her behalf. Consider the following comments when drafting the living will to conform it to the individual's beliefs of Islam.

Heroic Measures

The use of heroic measures under Islamic religious principles, according to at least one Islamic scholar, may be required if, according to the physician, a reasonable probability exists that the individual will survive with a reasonable quality of life. However, since the question of whether heroic measures may arise only when the person is in a severe vegetative state or the like, it would seem that heroic measures in such instances are not required.

Who Should Be Designated as Agent?

Under Islamic law, according to one Islamic scholar, the agent who should make the decisions may be required to be the parents, regardless of their ages, because of the significance and importance Islam affords a person's parents. Consult several imams (religious scholars/leaders) for clarification. The Islamic Society of North America (ISNA) may be able to provide forms and further clarification.

Definition of Death

While modern medicine may consider a person deceased when he or she registers a flat line electroencephalogram, that is, brain death, the issue may not be certain under Islamic religious principles. Consult several imams for clarification. The ISNA may be able to provide further clarification.

Organ Donations

Organ donation seems to be somewhat of a gray area. At least one Islamic scholar indicated that interpretations of the Koran allow organ donations. Another scholar noted that in religion human life is paramount, and everything should be done to perpetuate it. This scholar also stated that a person should ideally make the decision while competent. If that is not possible, the family should make that decision, and if there is no family, another person should make the decision on behalf of the potential donor. Another opinion, cited on ShiaNews.com in an article by ActiveIslam.com, is that organ donations from a deceased Muslim are allowed only to another Muslim if his or her life depends on it. Donations to non-Muslims are prohibited. Because there are a multitude of opinions on the matter, consult several imams for clarification. The ISNA may be able to provide further information.

Pregnancy

One Islamic scholar believes that the life of the mother takes precedence. Ideally, if the unborn child can be saved, whatever is necessary to save it should be done, but not at the expense of the mother's life. If the life of the unborn must be sacrificed to save the mother, as difficult as that may be, that would be the proper course of action.

Respect of the Deceased

In Islam, there is a strong belief not to do anything that desecrates the body. The corpse is surrounded by loved ones, who recite prayers for the deceased for swift entry into the world to come. The body is not left alone during the time period until burial. The body is put into the ground without a coffin. Some try to bury the body facing Mecca. Before the deceased is covered with dirt, a family member or religious person recites the *Shahadah* (the Muslim profession of faith that there is no God but Allah and no prophet but Muhammad) into the corpse's ear one last time.

ORTHODOX CHRISTIAN CONSIDERATIONS

The Orthodox Christian Church (includes all Eastern Orthodox churches, Greek, Russian, Antiocian, etc.) developed in the eastern portion of the Roman empire, and, as such, many congregants are from the Middle East (Lebanon, Syria, Israel) and the Greek-speaking parts of the world (Greece, Cyprus, Turkey) as well as Russia, Ukraine, Poland, Romania, and so on.

General Issues

Living wills and health care proxies raise a host of religious issues. What are some concerns that attorneys helping Orthodox Christians should address? The Church's view of life and death issues should ideally be reflected in the living will and health care proxy. A major tenant of the faith is that it is unethical to take a life. It is not the highest of all values to stay alive, but you cannot affirmatively take steps to kill someone. The Church is strongly against euthanasia and suicide. But often if the patient and medical care providers permit nature to take its course without heroic intervention, the person's life may be taken by God. So it is a narrow path. Taking a life is inappropriate. On the other hand, using heroic medical measures to keep a body biologically functioning is not appropriate either. Mere biological existence itself is not considered to be a value. It is not a sin to allow someone to die peacefully and with dignity. Death is seen as an end to be transformed into a victory by faith in God. The difficulty is discussing these issues in abstraction; they must be addressed on a case-by-case basis.

Because it has become so common in today's society for family members to intermarry and/or adopt different faiths, it is especially important that an individual's religious beliefs not be left unstated "because the family knows." They often don't. The following comment could be inserted into a living will to affirm affiliation with the Church and its basic values:

Sample Language: My Orthodox Christian beliefs hold that it is unethical to take a life. While it is not the highest of all values to preserve life, affirmative steps to cause death, including but not limited to euthanasia or suicide, are inappropriate. It can be permissible, and even appropriate in some circumstances, to allow nature to take its course without heroic medical intervention, until God determines to take my life. Using heroic medical measures to merely maintain my body's biological functioning is not appropriate since mere biological existence itself is not considered to be of value. My death, if with dignity and proper observance and respect for the rites and traditions of the Church, can be a victory of faith.

Pain Relief

Orthodox Christians affirm the act of suffering. It can be an experience providing purification, redemption, and salvation. However, they do not encourage suffering—steps can and should be taken to alleviate suffering. The religion teaches to alleviate suffering, but holds that suffering cannot be alleviated by taking a life.

A provision governing pain relief included in many living wills should be modified to reflect these important near-death wishes. Consider the following:

Sample Provision: Provide pain relief to the extent permissible according to Eastern Orthodox Christian doctrine: I wish that all treatment and measures for my comfort, and to alleviate my pain, be provided, so long as they do not rise to the level of constituting euthanasia. In making decisions concerning the administration of pain relief, I request that consideration be given to my Orthodox Christian beliefs and, in particular, the importance of my having some level of consciousness prior to death to be able to participate in accepting the holy communion and making a final confession of sin, as well as participating in certain prescribed prayer services. I request that my health care agent and medical care providers endeavor to humanely and compassionately balance my desire for pain relief and my desire to participate in my last religious observances.

Near-Death Issues

Much of the decision about consciousness and near-death traditions has to do with lucidity. Orthodox Christians should make provisions in advance by specifying their wishes in a living will and telling their family. The living will should state that they wish to have a priest present before death since there are many profound and moving prayers and observances for such a time. These traditions can bring great comfort to the patient and loved ones.

The entire process of dying is sanctified by a series of prayer services and sacraments. It is very important that the patient be lucid and free to confess his or her sins and to receive Holy Communion. The need for consciousness to participate in these sacraments should be considered when administering pain medication. There is also the rite of anointing a person with holy oil for healing of soul and body. Selected prayers are read throughout the illness: as suffering increases, as death nears, and after the person expires. For example, when a person is in great pain and approaching death, the priest may say the "Prayer of Separation of Soul and Body," asking God to take the life of the person and help him or her die in peace. Faithful members of the family are encouraged to be present during these prayers. The priest may also read a prayer immediately upon death.

The desire to have a priest present to say these prayers and to administer the sacraments should be communicated in the living will. If the family is not present and the living will does not inform the medical care providers, spiritual needs and wishes could be overlooked. In addition, if the children or other family members do not have the same religious beliefs, they may not know of these rites and traditions or that the person was among the faithful.

It seems essential that a priest be called to administer these rites and address the decisions since many of the issues to be decided are gray areas. In addition, the traditions are rich and require time. When drafting the living will, consider designating a particular priest or church to be contacted and providing contact numbers in the living will. The following example of a useful directive to indicate a priest or church addresses these decisions:

Sample Provision: Religious principles shall apply to the interpretation of this living will: I wish to condition the effectiveness of this directive on its conforming to Orthodox Christian doctrines and beliefs to which I subscribe. To effectuate my wishes, if any question arises as to the requirements of my religious beliefs, I direct that my health care agent consult with and follow the guidance of [insert name and telephone number of the priest] or if not available [insert name and telephone number of an alternate priest and/or the Church].

Definition of Death and Organ Donations

Orthodox Christians have no theological problems with organ donations as long as those involved are not trafficking in payments for organs or taking a life to obtain the organ. There is generally no problem from a religious perspective. Many pastors do, in fact, encourage organ donations out of compassion for those in need.

One of the issues many religions have been grappling with, however, is the definition of death. If you cannot take a life to harvest an organ, the definition of death is vital because removing an organ too early could be the cause of death. Generally, if life support were removed and the patient died, although it is a gray area from a religious perspective, it is unlikely to be an ethical problem to harvest organs at that time. Ethical experts would probably use the modern medical test of cessation of brainstem activity (brain death) as a definition of death.

Informing the Patient

It is critical that the patient have complete information about his or her condition; otherwise, the patient will never be able to know when to begin the many important religious observances that are to accompany the process of dying. The following is an example of a directive that could be integrated into the living will to express the patient's wishes as he or she nears death:

Sample Clause: Wishes concerning knowledge of my condition: I specifically direct my agent and all attending medical personnel to fully and completely inform me and my agent of my medical condition, including but not limited to the fact that I may have a terminal illness, and my anticipated life expectancy. This information is vital to my carrying out important religious practices as an Orthodox Christian.

CHRISTIAN SCIENTIST CONSIDERATIONS

Adherents of the Church of Christ Scientist (Christian Science) believe that healing occurs through the realization of God's allness, goodness, power, and presence. Illness can be overcome through the power of the divine mind and God. Although Christian Scientists typically choose prayer for healing themselves and their children, individuals are free to choose whatever from of treatment or care they feel will best answer their needs. While it may be customary that they pray for themselves, they may call a Christian Science practitioner. Christian Scientists should expressly address adherence to Christian Science beliefs and specifically request care by a Christian Science nurse in their living will, if that is their wish.

Consider language similar to the following to include in the preamble of the living will:

Sample Clause: I am an adherent to the Church of Christ Scientists (Christian Science) and believe that healing derives from reflecting the false concept in favor of the trust. I believe that by turning human thought to the enlightening and saving power of the divine trust of God, healing will result from drawing close to God. In the event of illness or disease, my preference and wish is to have a Christian Science nurse and, if appropriate, the assistance of a Christian Science practitioner or lay reader, rather than be given medication and medical intervention. Further, by way of example and not limitation, my preference is to accept a vaccine only if required by law and that drugs and blood products not be given to me. Given my wish to have only permitted Christian Science treatments, I request that in the event of my illness, to the extent feasible, I be cared for in my home or in a Christian Science sanatorium or care facility. I expressly authorize the cessation or nonprovision of any medical care, surgical treatment, including, by way of example, the use of a ventilator, CPR, or feeding tube. I do not believe in euthanasia.

Since the Church does not coerce or pressure members who choose to avail themselves of medical treatment, it is vital to address the extent to which the individual does or does not wish medical treatment. Should he or she be given palliative care? Pain relief? To what extent?

JEHOVAH'S WITNESS CONSIDERATIONS

Since a Jehovah Witness's living will has specific instructions that differ markedly from what many other people would expect, they should clearly label their living wills as demanding care in conformity with the tenants of Jehovah Witnesses to alert medical staff: "Application of living will in accordance with religious tenants of a Jehovah's Witness." The use of blood products in many medical procedures creates a host of problems for the Jehovah's Witness, and these issues may not be known or anticipated by medical care providers.

The following sample clauses are intended to comply with the religious principles of Jehovah's Witnesses as to many issues, for example, blood transfusions, heroic measures, and end-of-life decisions. Be certain to consult with the elders of the Church to review the appropriateness of these provisions and to determine whether other special arrangements may be necessary. It may be advisable for Jehovah's Witnesses, when traveling, to determine in advance if medical facilities capable of following the religious tenants are available.

Sample Clause: I am a Jehovah's Witness. I clearly and expressly state that because of my religious beliefs (based in part on the provisions of Acts 15:28 and 29), I do not wish to have homologous blood transfusion or even autologous blood (my own stored blood) under any and all circumstances, no matter what my medical condition. This restriction shall apply to any type and manner of blood or blood product (platelets or plasma). This restriction shall apply regardless of medical experts or other health care providers stating that blood transfusion is essential to preserve my life or the life of my unborn fetus.

I may be given nonblood alternatives to regenerate my own blood, to minimize blood loss, to replace lost circulatory volume, or to stop bleeding. These may include, by way of example, volume expanders such as dextran, saline or Ringer's solution, or hetastarch.

I may be treated in a manner that results in the dilution of my blood within an extracorporeal circuit that does not involve storage or more than a brief interruption of blood flow and that is constantly linked to my circulatory system. I also will accept contemporaneous recovery and reinfusion of blood lost during or after surgery that does not involve storage for more than brief interruption of my blood flow. However, in no event may any equipment used in such treatments contain any blood products or remnants.

The prohibitions against blood transfusions may or may not be defined to include other related products, which might contain blood products. Therefore, the living will should clarify the following items by expressly stating that the individual wishes to be given them if medically indicated or not given even if they are medically indicated. Each item should be discussed with a physician knowledgeable in treating Jehovah's Witnesses, as well as with the Church elders:

- Albumin, which is a protein that can be used for fluid resuscitation to temporize the condition if blood pressure drops; it is used in some radionuclide scan preparations.
- Streptokinase, which is used to dissolve blood clots.
- Recombinant products, which are artificially made from viruses that replicate human DNA, such as erythropoietin (EPO), a hormone made by the kidney that may allow the body to make more red blood cells and synthesized clotting factors.

- Immunoglobulins, which can be given to build immunity. This might include Rh immune globulin (during pregnancy if the patient is Rh negative and has a fetus that is Rh positive), gammaglobulin (if exposed to a virus for which the patient did not receive a vaccine), and so on.
- Clotting factors, such as fibrinogen, a protein the body makes in clot formation.

QUESTIONS TO CONSIDER

1. Are you religious? Are your agents? Family?
2. Would you find solace by turning to religion in trying times?
3. Would you want your decisions influenced by your religious beliefs?
4. Should mechanical means of prolonging life be used?
5. Do you wish to have artificial feeding? Would you permit artificial feeding to be withdrawn even if discontinuing it could hasten death?
6. What are your feelings and wishes about health care, treatment, quality of life, and whether you may wish to refuse or accept medical treatment?
7. Organ donations are a vital step to help save the lives of others. Seriously and carefully give thought to permitting organ donations.
8. Do you wish any specific eulogy, service, or steps be taken? Do you want a traditional religious ceremony?
9. Do you have definite religious convictions? A definite lack of them?
10. What about pain medication and other treatments or procedures to reduce pain? Should they be administered even if they hasten death? Are there adverse religious implications if pain relief hastens death?
11. Do you know what your religion says about these various issues? Do you care?

12. Is there a particular religious authority to whom you are close and with whom you would want to discuss these issues?

13. Are there any religious ceremonies you want performed?

CHAPTER SUMMARY

Indicating your religious preference in your living will is essential to those wishes being made known and being carried out. As our society has become more complex, eclectic, and diverse, it is wrong to assume that health care providers and, in many cases, even family will understand your religious beliefs. Clarifying your beliefs in reasonable detail is important. This chapter provided an overview of some of the issues raised by eight different religions. Whatever religion you adhere to (or that your loved ones might assume you do) should be addressed.

5 HEALTH CARE PROXIES

WHAT IS A HEALTH CARE PROXY AND WHY DO YOU NEED ONE?

A health care proxy, also called a health care power of attorney, is a formal legal document in which you designate a person to make medical and related decisions for you. This person is called your *agent*. Your agent will be given authority to make decisions only if you cannot do so for yourself. This is one of the most important steps to protect your end-of-life and other medical decisions. A health care proxy appointing a person to act as your agent is important because the myriad possible decisions that might have to be made can never be anticipated in advance. Appointing an agent authorized to act, with the full knowledge of the facts that exist at some future date, is the most flexible way to address the uncertainty. Your health care proxy should specify your agents and the powers or rights you intend them to have. This chapter explains many of the options and decisions available to you.

WHY YOU NEED A HEALTH CARE PROXY IN ADDITION TO YOUR LIVING WILL

The health care proxy is essential to provide you with protection because it offers a mechanism for decisions to be made by your agent, your chosen representative, if, when, and where the need exists. Your living will, discussed in preceding chapters, should set forth general parameters for your wishes, but at the time a specific decision needs to be made, an agent can react to the specific circumstances. Naming a health care agent is essential when the parameters contained in your living will are too vague or general, which usually happens with most simplistic forms.

Example: Sally Martin's living will states that if she is in a persistent vegetative state, she does not wish to have heroic measures taken. The phrase "persistent vegetative state" can probably be clinically demonstrated by a neurologist if it can be documented that there is no higher order brain function (e.g., cortical brain function) by various tests perhaps including an electroencephalogram (EEG). However, how should the term *heroic measures* be defined? Assume that Sally's living will is silent as to additional details. Without the input of an agent, it might be impossible to define this subjective term. If Sally is devoutly religious, inserting a feeding tube would not be considered a heroic measure. In fact, for Sally, with a religious worldview, providing nutrition may be viewed as mandatory. Failing to provide nutrition would be equivalent to starving Sally and tantamount to murder in her view. Without an agent's input, Sally's attending physicians couldn't know this.

Another option to Sally's situation is for her to have specified her religious beliefs in her living will. While this might have avoided the need for an agent's intervention in the preceding example, it is but one example. Myriad other situations could arise.

Example: John Smith's living will states that if he is terminally ill, he does not wish to have heroic measures taken. The terminology is vague and subjective, so it is necessary for an agent to make an interpretation. John is terminally ill with inoperable lung cancer. His prognosis is a few months. John develops, while in the hospital, a pocket of infection in his large colon (diverticular abscess), for which he is placed on antibiotics. The abscess perforates and the decision must be made to operate. Is treating this infection "heroic"? If John is not treated, the infection will reach his blood stream and cause death. Should surgical intervention occur to give John the chance to live out his last few months before the inoperable lung cancer causes his death? Is the surgery a heroic measure, which John's living will requests that he not have? If surgery is not performed and John is treated merely for the pain, his death might occur sooner. Is this preferable? If John is treated for the abscess, he will remain terminally ill. His last days may be spent on a respirator in the intensive care unit (ICU). Is this a preferable way to die? Should surgery be authorized? John's age and a host of other factors might be relevant to the decision. But without the appointment of an agent, the literal reading of John's living will, especially the "no heroic measures" language, might be interpreted in a manner different from what John would have wanted. Precious time might be lost.

Even if you make efforts to be clear and precise in your living will, it is impossible to foresee every possible future illness, every possible treatment your physicians may prescribe, or every possible eventuality that must be addressed. By appointing a person to act in your behalf, the decisions that cannot be foreseen and addressed in your living will can be made by an agent at that future time when they must be dealt with. Your agent makes decisions based on your condition at that future time, with consideration to the then-available medical procedures and advice and your wishes as he or she interprets them.

If naming an agent is so important, why do you also need a living will setting forth your health care wishes? The living will, if properly done, can serve to inform your agent of your wishes, for example, your general religious beliefs, your desire not to have heroic measures if you are terminally ill, and so forth. Even if your agent knows your wishes, stating clearly in writing that you do not wish to be kept alive or that you do not wish every measure to be taken to save you relieves your agents of some of the trauma from making a decision to forgo ordering every medical measure. Many family members, when acting as agents, order medical steps to be taken out of guilt, rather than from the perspective of what the loved one would really need or want. Your giving permission to forgo any procedures relieves some of this guilt. In addition, a detailed living will can provide invaluable advice if you don't have someone to name as agent or your agent cannot be reached.

Example: At 2:00 A.M. on a Sunday morning during a winter storm, not every agent can be reached. But a living will in your medical records can provide some detail.

Chapter 2 addresses the need for an agent in the context of living wills.

WHOM SHOULD YOU NAME AS YOUR HEALTH CARE AGENT?

The decision as to whom to appoint is often very difficult. Some of your loved ones, even if sensitive to your feelings, may simply not be emotionally capable to make the very difficult decisions that could become necessary. Is it fair for you to burden them with this responsibility?

Do not necessarily assume that the person you select will be able to carry out your wishes. Many people simply do not have the emotional composition to deal with the difficult emotional, medical, and personal issues that might arise. Prospective agents may have religious, moral, or other personal reasons for not being willing to carry out certain wishes. Some people have suffered through difficult end-of-life decisions with other loved ones and might not wish to face the trauma again. Others may have found knowledge and experience through such events and are better able to serve. Discuss these important matters with every agent or successor agent in advance. Request their permission. Respect their decisions.

Religious considerations may also play a role in deciding who your agent should be.

Choosing Your Spouse as Your Agent

Although the most natural agent for many is their spouse, this decision should not be automatic. If your marriage is relatively new, it is not uncommon to name a parent or other family member as your agent. If you feel you should name someone other than your spouse, however, it's essential that you sign a health care proxy appointing someone else. Otherwise, the likely assumption is that your spouse is your choice.

If you name your spouse, what happens if you separate or divorce? You might wish to consider including the following paragraph:

Sample Clause: If my spouse has been designated as an agent or alternate agent hereunder, and if subsequent to the execution of this document, my spouse and I are legally separated or divorced, any rights and powers granted to my spouse shall immediately terminate on such legal separation or divorce.

If you think you'd like to include similar language in your health care proxy, consider the impact on a hospital. Does the clause mean that in an emergency, the hospital must verify that your spouse hasn't commenced divorce proceedings?

Don't Assume a Child Is the Right Choice

Be very careful in naming a child to make decisions. Many children, even those who have long ago passed the age of majority, have a very difficult time in making a "pull the plug" decision for a parent. If you name your children as agents, can they really bear this responsibility? It is usually inadvisable to name a child under age 25 to handle this difficult decision.

If you have more than one child, do you name all? Do you name one or the other? As mentioned later, some states prohibit joint agents.

Name More than One Agent

Don't name only one agent. You should name additional agents to serve in the event the first (or prior) named agent cannot serve. These agents are called *successor* agents.

Don't Name Joint Agents

It is recommended that you never require joint action by two or more people to make a decision as agents. Be careful to name the agents to serve successively, that is, to act individually and independently, not jointly. Thus, the second can serve only if the first cannot, but they don't make decisions together.

No medical care provider wants to be caught between two joint agents with different opinions on what should be done. If one of two joint agents is not available, a medical provider might not accept the decision of only one agent. Some state laws prohibit the appointment of a joint agent, doing so might invalidate your document.

If you wish to name two people, consider instead naming them sequentially but add nonbinding language to the health care proxy suggesting, but not requiring, that the agents consult with each other if feasible before acting. This avoids joint decision making but makes clear to your agents (e.g., your two children) that they should consult with each other. It's not ideal, but it might be a sufficient compromise to accomplish your goals without jeopardizing the efficacy of your health care proxy document.

If you suggest that the agent consult with others before acting, consider including language similar to the following to make it clear to any medical provider that consulting with others is merely a request, not a binding legal requirement creating an obligation:

Sample Clause: I request, but do not require, that any agent appointed above endeavor to consult with other appointed successor agents, where feasible, prior to taking any action.

Appointing Alternate Co-Agents

If you have, for example, two children and want them both to be appointed, you might wish to name both as agents. To avoid the difficulty of requiring two signatures to approve any action, you might wish to authorize medical providers to accept the decision of either. As noted in the preceding discussion, this is not a recommended approach because of the problems it can create. However, if it is valid in your state and you wish to pursue it, discuss it with your attorney. You could appoint more than one person as co-agent. You might, instead of requiring agreement of both (or all) agents, authorize either agent to act without the requirement of joint action:

Sample Clause: I expressly authorize any health care provider to rely on the authorization or decision of either of such co-agents, with no requirement to seek approval or consent from the other of such agents. The appointment under this paragraph is not intended to create joint agents. If only one of the above named agents is able or willing to serve, such person shall continue to serve alone as my sole agent.

The last sentence of the clause addresses the situation of one of your two joint agents being incapacitated, unavailable, or deceased and not being able to act. If the remaining agent isn't authorized to act alone, after all your efforts you would have no agent to act. This precaution, however, also points out another problem of the multiple agent approach. How could a medical provider determine that the other agent is not available?

WHAT DETAILS ABOUT YOUR AGENTS SHOULD YOU INCLUDE IN YOUR HEALTH CARE PROXY?

You need to appoint each agent in your health care proxy, providing his or her full legal name. If the agent has a nickname or is known by several names (such as a maiden and married name), list all names in the document so that if a medical provider requests identification from the agent, his or her identification will be consistent with one of the several names listed in your health care proxy. You should also list each agent's complete address and telephone numbers, including daytime and evening, cell phone, and, if applicable, pager number. In the event of a medical emergency, having all likely numbers may be the key to medical staff reaching your agent quickly or even at all.

IF NONE OF THE PEOPLE NAMED AS AGENT CAN SERVE

The best precaution against your agent's not being able to serve is to name several alternate or succeeding agents to serve, in the order you list, if the prior-named agents are unable to do so. However, not everyone has a long list of agents; and even if several agents are named, it is possible that none may be available to act. One way to address this eventuality is to have a living will advising medical providers of your wishes if no agent can. An additional precaution is to vest in the medical providers the right to make decisions based on your living will. While this provision may not be accepted, it might provide an additional safeguard:

Sample Language: If all of the above agents have predeceased me or are unable or unwilling for any reason to serve as my agent, but an agent is required by law solely in order to direct the withholding or withdrawal of life-sustaining treatment or other medical or health care objectives in accordance with my wishes, I authorize my attending physician to appoint such an agent upon consultation with one or more of my relatives, religious advisers (if any are specified herein), friends, or other persons or agencies reasonably believed to be interested in my well-being.

POWERS AND AUTHORITY TO GIVE YOUR HEALTH CARE AGENT

What authority should your health care proxy give to your agents? You need to achieve a balance of granting sufficiently detailed power to your agent to enable him or her to act, but at the same time you need to be general and broad enough that your agent can address unanticipated and unforeseeable issues. The following discussion is an overview; Chapter 6 provides a more detailed analysis of powers and authority.

Do you wish to authorize your agent to execute a "Do not resuscitate" (DNR) or "No code" order? Such an order authorizes the medical staff not to institute life support measures in the event of a cardiac or respiratory arrest. You might wish to specify a DNR if you are terminally ill (a condition from which there is no hope of recovery) and you suffer from chronic pain or if you are in a persistent vegetative state with no meaningful hope of recovery. In other conditions, you may not wish to authorize a DNR. Most health care proxies are general and simply authorize the right for the agent to execute a DNR order and leave to your living will the details concerning the parameters for when a DNR should be issued.

You might wish to authorize your agent to give or withhold consent to any medical procedure, test, or treatment, including surgery.

Too often the media has focused attention on merely the right to cease life support or heroic measures; however, other issues beyond this limited scope often require attention. Your health care proxy should be a broad grant of authority, not limited to merely making so-called end-of-life decisions. These additional powers or rights granted to your agent could include the right to arrange for your convalescent care, hospice care, or home care. You might wish to authorize your agent to make arrangements for companion care or other steps. If you prefer to stay in your own home or, alternatively, to be in a facility with other people with whom you might mingle, you should make that known in the way that you grant powers to your agent.

You should authorize your agent to make funeral arrangements—address details for a service, burial or cremation, and interment—and other details that you wish.

READ YOUR STATE'S HEALTH CARE PROXY LAW

Even if you hire an estate planning specialist in your state to review and guide you on the final preparation (drafting) and signing (execution) of your health care proxy, which is recommended, you should take the time to read your state's law (statute) covering (governing) health care proxies. Reading the law will give you a much better understanding of what is involved, what issues you should address in your health care proxy, and how gaps in your health care proxy might be interpreted or filled in by your state's law.

State Name	Law (Statute) Reference	Specific Sections (§§) of the Law
Alabama	Alabama Code	22-8A-1 to 22-8A-10
Alaska	Alaska Statute	13.26.355
Arizona	Arizona Revised Statute Annotated	14-5312
Arkansas	Arkansas Code Annotated	20-13-901 to 20-13-908
California	Probate Code	4606-4752 and 4770-4779
Colorado	Colorado Revised Statute	15-18-101 to 15-18-113
Connecticut	Connecticut General Statute	19A-570 to 19A-580c
Delaware	Delaware Code Annotated Title 16	2503 to 2509
District of Columbia	District of Columbia Code Annotated	21-2201 to 21-2213
Florida	Florida Statute Chapter	765.301 et seq.
Georgia	Georgia Code Annotated	31-36-1 to 31-36-13
Hawaii	Hawaii Revised Statute	327D-1 et seq.
Illinois	Illinois Revised Statute	755 et seq.
Indiana	Indiana Code	16-36-4-1 to 16-36-4-21
Iowa	Iowa Code	144A.1 et seq.
Kansas	Kansas Statute Annotated	65-28.101 et seq.
Louisiana	Louisiana Revised Statute Annotated	40:1299.58.1 et seq.
Maine	Maine Revised Statute Annotated Title 18-A	5-701 et seq.
Maryland	Maryland Code Annotated Health-General	5-601 to 5-618
Massachusetts	Massachusetts General Law Chapter 201D	1 et seq.
Michigan	Michigan Compilation Laws	700.496 et seq.
Minnesota	Minnesota Statute	145C.01 et seq.
Mississippi	Mississippi Code Annotated	41-41-101 et seq.
Missouri	Missouri Revised Statute	459.010 et seq.
Montana	Montana Code Annotated	50-9-101 et seq.
Nebraska	Nebraska Revised Statute	30-3401 et seq.
Nevada	Nevada Revised Statute	449.535-690 and 449.800-860

State Name	Law (Statute) Reference	Specific Sections (§§) of the Law
New Hampshire	New Hampshire Revised Statute Annotated	137-H:1 et seq.
New Jersey	New Jersey Revised Statute	26:2H-53
New Mexico	New Mexico Statute Annotated	24-7-1 to 24-7-10
New York	New York Public Health Law	2980 et seq.
North Carolina	North Carolina General Statute	32A-15 to 32A-26
North Dakota	North Dakota Central Code	23-06.5-01 to 23-06.5-18
Ohio	Ohio Revised Code Annotated	2133.01 et seq.
Oklahoma	Oklahoma Statute Title 43A	11-101 et seq.
Oregon	Oregon Revised Statute	127.505 et seq.
Pennsylvania	Pennsylvania Connotated Statute Annotated	540 et seq.
Rhode Island	Rhode Island General Laws	23-4.10-1 to 23-4.10-12
South Carolina	South Carolina Code Annotated	44-77-10 et seq.
South Dakota	South Dakota Codified Laws Annotated	34-12C-1 to 34-12C-8
Tennessee	Tennessee Code Annotated	34-6-101 et seq.
Texas	Texas Health & Safety Code Annotated	672.001 et seq.
Utah	Utah Code Annotated	75-2-1101 et seq.
Vermont	Vermont Statute Annotated Title 14	3463 et seq.
Virginia	Virginia Code Annotated	54.1-2981 to 54.1-2993
Washington	Washington Revised Code	70.122.010 et seq.
West Virginia	West Virginia Code	16-30B-1 et seq.
Wisconsin	Wisconsin Statute	155.01 et seq.
Wyoming	Wyoming Statute	35-22-100

QUESTIONS TO CONSIDER

1. What is the relationship of your health care proxy to your living will?

2. Is there someone in particular whom you feel comfortable with making these important health care decisions for you? Is this person willing and able to act?

3. Does the person you've named as agent know your views on different issues such as religion, quality of life, and other fundamental personal views?

4. Does the agent have beliefs similar to yours concerning certain medical procedures? If not, even if the agent understands your wishes, will the agent have the sensitivity and willingness to act if he or she has very different beliefs?

5. What types of issues do you want to entrust to your agent? Should some decisions be specified in absolute terms and with clarity in your living will and your agent be simply directed to follow those wishes?

6. Do you have alternate agents in case the person you've chosen isn't able to fulfill his or her responsibility or in case of death of the agent?

7. Have you addressed any current medical conditions with your physicians to be certain that your agent is given direction?

8. Would you permit your agent ever to withdraw artificial nutrition and hydration?

CHAPTER SUMMARY

Health care proxies are a vital component to your end-of-life decisions. You need to coordinate the decisions in your health care proxy in terms of the rights and powers you give your agent to the parameters of your wishes listed in your living will. When you prepare your living will, you hope to plan for most foreseeable future medical contingencies, but since it is impossible to foresee all possibilities, you need to appoint an agent who will decide for you. Who will make the decision to order a DNR or if and when to approve a particular treatment? Who will decide where you will be buried or what type of service you will have? If you made arrangements in advance, you still should authorize an agent to implement these decisions. Your health care proxy should empower and authorize a person, your agent, to make these decisions for you.

6 DETAILED CLAUSES TO CONSIDER INCLUDING IN YOUR HEALTH CARE PROXY

INTRODUCTION TO DETAILED HEALTH CARE PROXY DECISIONS

If you wish to provide for the management of your person, body, health, and medical affairs in a more orderly fashion, you need to appoint an agent (attorney-in-fact) to act on your behalf. Whether it is simple or difficult for you to designate the person to act on your behalf, there remain a host of specific decisions to make concerning the powers for your agent.

POWERS TO GIVE YOUR HEALTH CARE AGENT

You want to grant your agent all the powers and rights necessary to effect your wishes.

General Statement of Powers to Do Any Act You Can

You generally want to give your agent the full power and authority to do, take, and perform each and every act whatsoever required, proper, or necessary to carry out your health care wishes. This should include any right your state's laws make available to an agent acting in such capacity. Effectively, you want to grant to your agent the authority to act as fully and for all reasons and purposes as you might or could act if you were personally able to do so. A general statement of power for your agent can be important in case a specific decision arises for which you did not give your agent the authority to act. If the state law provides the right for an agent to address the issue, state law might fill in the gap in your health care proxy. For example, if you didn't define "heroic measures," state law definitions may then be used.

Your agent should be entitled to sign, execute, deliver, and acknowledge any contract or other document that may be necessary, desirable, convenient, or proper to exercise any of the powers described in your health care proxy and to incur reasonable costs in the exercise of any such powers.

Grant of Medical Decisions Powers

You should specifically designate your agent to make medical treatment decisions for you if you are comatose or otherwise unable to make such decisions for yourself, including any decisions with respect to life-sustaining measures, artificial feeding, artificial hydration, and other matters.

Do Not Resuscitate (DNR)

You might wish to authorize your agent to sign or approve a "Do not resuscitate" or "No code" order. This authorizes your agent to direct your attending personnel not to resuscitate you in the event of a cardiac or respiratory arrest.

Consent to or Disapprove Treatment

You should also authorize your agent to give or withhold consent for any medical procedure, test, or treatment, including surgery. The agent should have authority to act within the directions you have given in your living will. The grant of authority to your agent to approve or disapprove medical procedures and care should be broad to permit flexibility to make the decision based on the advice of your attending physician with consideration to your medical condition at the time. As examples throughout this book illustrate, the decision to approve many medical procedures is a gray area that requires judgment.

The authority to approve or disapprove medical procedures might include the right to summon paramedics or other emergency medical personnel and seek emergency treatment when needed or to restrict such emergency treatment by paramedics or other emergency medical procedures. Ambulance and other emergency medical personnel won't generally consider a living will or health care proxy because their mission is to take emergency steps to address whatever medical crisis you are facing, not to review legal documents.

Your agent may also, depending on your personal religious, moral, and other views, be authorized to withdraw, modify, or change consent for any medical procedure, test, hospitalization, or other treatment that either you or your agent may have arranged. While naming an agent and authorizing an agent to address such issues are recommended, they don't always guarantee a smooth decision process.

Case Study

John Smith was born into a Jehovah's Witness family but married outside the faith. Jehovah's Witnesses have strong beliefs against the use and administration of blood and blood products. John signed a health care proxy and named his wife, Cindy Smith, as agent. Tragically, John is in a car accident and rushed to the local hospital. The family arrives. The physicians inform the family that John needs emergency surgery to survive. Cindy is ready to authorize the blood infusion necessary to conduct the surgery. The family argues that John has strict religious beliefs that prohibit the use of blood, which must be considered. John's living will and health care proxy are silent as to religious beliefs. Cindy argues that John has long ago moved away from the faith and would want every measure taken to save his life. The family argues to the contrary that the restrictions of a Jehovah's Witness are exactly what John wants. Although a Jehovah's Witness may allow treatment when the dilution of blood in an extracorporeal circuit does not involve storage or more than a brief interruption of blood flow and is constantly linked to his circulatory system, this procedure may present greater risk. What should be done? The family may truly believe that John has remained faithful and wishes his faith respected. Cindy may truly know that John has moved away from the faith and would not wish any restrictions on his medical procedures. Is it possible that John has remained faithful, but Cindy sees an opportunity to hurt a family that has never fully welcomed her?

"Since Cindy was named agent, the medical professionals would follow the wife's instructions as agent unless they felt she were acting in bad faith," observes Margaret Galvin, vice president of legal affairs at Holy Name Hospital in Teaneck, New Jersey. The better choice is to be precise and address in detail to what extent you want a particular religious belief recognized in your treatment.

Palliative and Related Care

Your agent should be authorized to make all necessary arrangements for you at any hospital, hospice, nursing home (including veterans' nursing care facility or any state- or federally run facility), convalescent home, or similar establishment. This includes your transfer and removal and ensures that all your essential needs are provided for at such a facility.

You should also authorize your agent to provide for companionship that will meet your needs and preferences when you are disabled or otherwise unable to arrange for such companionship yourself.

In addition, your agent's authority should include employment and discharge of medical personnel, including physicians, psychiatrists, dentists, nurses, and therapists as your agent deems necessary for your physical, mental, and emotional well-being.

Moving You to Another Facility

If the hospital or medical care facility will not carry out your wishes, you may wish to authorize your agent to transfer you to a facility where your wishes can or will be carried out. In light of the significant variations in state law, you might wish to authorize your removal to another state. You should direct your health care providers to cooperate with and assist in promptly transferring you to another health care facility. Especially because of the many restrictions on the transferring of health care information, you should authorize and direct your medical care providers to transfer a copy of all of your medical records to any new facility. To encourage compliance with this request, you can indemnify the medical care facility releasing you and your records.

Implement Funeral, Burial, and Related Decisions Specified in Your Living Will

Your health care proxy should authorize your agent to make advance arrangements for the treatment of your remains as provided for in your living will. This could include the right to contract with a funeral home, cemetery, or other business or entity.

Some agents are authorized to address these issues for other family members and loved ones. This authorization might include the right to inquire as to whether the cemetery or cemeteries where your family are buried or interred are fulfilling their responsibilities under any applicable perpetual care contracts in existence and the right to take any actions to ensure that your wishes concerning these matters are carried out. You may also suggest and authorize your agent to direct the executor (personal administrator) under your last will and testament to make any reasonable payments toward the decisions made by your health care agent for these arrangements.

Arrange for Organ Donation Wishes

Organ donations should be discussed in detail with your agent if you wish to be a donor. If you do not wish to be an organ donor, that wish should be specifically communicated to your agent as well. You want your agent to carry out your wish to be an organ and tissue donor upon your death by informing the attending medical personnel that you are a donor. There may be papers to be executed or other acts necessary in connection with such gifts, and your agent must be empowered to act appropriately in these cases to make anatomical gifts that will take effect at your death.

Pain Relief

Your living will should specify your desires for pain relief and any philosophical, religious, or personal limitations on pain relief. Your health care proxy should authorize your agent to order whatever is appropriate to keep you as comfortable and free of pain as is reasonably possible, including the administration of pain-relieving drugs, surgical or medical procedures calculated to relieve your pain, and unconventional pain-relief therapies that your agent believes might be helpful.

To Serve as Your Guardian or Conservator

If you are incapable of making legal, medical, or other decisions for yourself, a court may have to appoint someone to act for you. You can use your health care proxy document to encourage a court to appoint the person you select to be your guardian. If you trust someone's judgment to carry out the decisions in your living will and to have the powers given in your health care proxy, it is likely that you would trust and choose the same person to act as a guardian if one should have to be appointed (see Chapter 7).

INDEMNIFICATION OF AGENT

You should agree to indemnify and hold harmless your agent (including any successor agent) for any actions taken, or not taken, if the agent acted in good faith and was not guilty of fraud, gross negligence, or willful misconduct. Most health care proxies don't include an indemnification of the agent. However, the objective is to encourage your agent to carry out your end-of-life wishes and protect your dignity. Fear of a lawsuit by family members or others should not inhibit your agent from taking the actions he or she knows you wish taken. An indemnification may help.

CONSTRUCTION AND INTERPRETATION OF THE HEALTH CARE PROXY

Your health care proxy is to be construed and interpreted as a durable general power of attorney for medical, health care, and related matters. The enumeration of specific items, rights, acts, or powers is not intended to limit or restrict, and is not to be construed or interpreted as limiting or restricting, the general powers granted to said agent.

Your health care proxy may be signed in one state but intended to be effective in a different state. It should clearly specify the state in which it was signed and the state law intended to govern its application.

If any provision or power in your living will is found by a court to be unenforceable, this finding should not adversely affect the enforceability of the rest of your health care proxy. You should specifically state that you have granted your agent authority and power over your health and personal matters to ensure the carrying out of your wishes. State that should this grant be prohibited by any law presently existing or hereinafter enacted, such grant should be interpreted in the broadest manner permitted by such law; and if such grant is prohibited, every other provision of your health care proxy should nevertheless remain fully valid and enforceable.

OTHER PEOPLE RELYING ON THE HEALTH CARE PROXY

Third parties, such as medical professionals, hospitals, convalescent facilities, nursing homes, hospices, or the like, may expressly be authorized to rely on the representations of your agent for all matters relating to your health care decisions. You should state that those representations of your agent or the authority granted to your agent shall not cause any liability to you or your estate as a result of permitting the agent to exercise any power conveyed in your health care proxy.

INSPECTION AND PHOTOCOPIES OF DOCUMENTS AND RECORDS

Your agent should have the authority to request and inspect any reports, files, or other records about your condition and should be authorized to execute documents, releases, or other approvals or prerequisites to such inspections.

Your agent should also be authorized to make photocopies of your health care proxy as necessary so that any third party may then rely on a duly executed counterpart of the instrument and a copy certified by your agent as being a true copy of the original.

Your agent should be empowered to request, receive, and review any information about your medical, physical, or mental health, including but not limited to hospital records, and to execute any release or other documents that may be required to obtain such information and to disclose such information to such persons, organizations, and others as your agent deems appropriate.

DISABILITY DOES NOT AFFECT VALIDITY OF THE HEALTH CARE PROXY

Your health care proxy should specifically state that it will not be invalidated by your later disability. In other words, it is your intention that all powers conferred on your agent shall remain at all times in full force and effect, regardless of your incapacity, disability, or any uncertainty.

RESIGNATION OF AGENT

Your health care proxy should provide a specific mechanism for your agent to resign if he or she doesn't wish to serve. It could specify that any agent may resign by providing written

notice to you or your guardian (you may need a court procedure to get one) if you are then incompetent.

SHOULD YOUR AGENT BE COMPENSATED?

No health care agent should receive compensation for the performance of the responsibilities as agent. Decisions made as an
agent should not be influenced by compensation, and compensation may raise questions as to the validity of your health care
proxy document. You might wish, however, to state that your
agent may be reimbursed for actual and necessary expenses incurred in the performance of his or her responsibilities.

COORDINATE FINANCIAL AND HEALTH CARE AGENTS

Financial documents, such as a durable power of attorney
and revocable living trust, should be coordinated with your living will and health care proxy. Often, the people designated as
having financial powers are different from the people making
health care decisions. You don't want those holding financial
powers to dictate medical decisions by refusing to fund the decisions made by a health care agent. One approach to addressing this issue is to have an express direction to the financial
agent in your financial power of attorney and to your trustee of
your revocable living trust to fund the health care decisions
made by the agent under your health care proxy. The agent appointed under the health care proxy should be instructed to cooperate with the financial agent under your financial power of
attorney (or the trustee under your revocable living trust if you
have one).

COPIES OF DOCUMENT

It is important to specify that a copy of your health care proxy
document should be as valid as the original because copies can

be required by the hospital, physician, rehabilitation locations, and so on. You can also recommend in the document that a copy be made part of your permanent medical record.

SEVERABILITY

Your health care proxy should state that its provisions are severable so that the invalidity of one or more provisions should not affect the validity of other provisions. Thus, if one of the wishes you have stated violates state law, the entire document should not be invalidated. This is important in light of the dynamic nature of the laws applying to health care proxies. It is particularly important if you have unusual health care wishes.

COMPETENCY TO EXECUTE DOCUMENT

For your health care proxy to be valid, you have to be competent when you sign it. Your health care proxy should state that you understand its full import and that you are emotionally and mentally competent to execute it.

SIGNATURE AND NOTARY LINES

As with any legal document, you should sign your health care proxy in the presence and under the supervision of an attorney in your state and in front of two witnesses and a notary public. The witnesses should be acquainted with you, believe you are of sound mind and under no constraint, duress, or undue influence. The witnesses should not be related to you by blood or marriage and should not be entitled to any portion of your estate in the event of your death. If they were, there could be an ulterior motive that makes their witnessing your health care proxy questionable. The witnesses should not be physicians attending to you as a patient. The witnesses should be over 18 years of age. Your health care proxy should state all of these facts.

QUESTIONS TO CONSIDER

1. Are you comfortable with the agents you have selected to act on your behalf? The successors?

2. Have you discussed with your proposed agents what your wishes are, and are you satisfied that they are in agreement with your desires?

3. Will the agent(s) you selected be able to stand firm with your desires if family members are not in agreement with them?

4. Have you reviewed with your physician how to address any current medical conditions in your health care proxy?

5. Should you indemnify your agent?

6. Have you reviewed with a lawyer in your state technical matters that should be addressed in your health care proxy to ensure that it complies with state law?

CHAPTER SUMMARY

A health care proxy is an instrument legally appointing an agent to act on your behalf. It authorizes the agent to act on your behalf and directs him or her to make certain decisions for you. Review your current medical conditions, living will, and general wishes to be certain to grant your agent the powers necessary to carry out your health care wishes. Be certain to address a broad array of wishes, not only the end-of-life medical decisions. Sign and notarize the instrument in accordance with any formalities that apply in your state.

7 GUARDIANSHIP: WHAT IT IS AND HOW YOU MAY AVOID IT

WHAT IS GUARDIANSHIP?

If you are unable to make personal and/or financial decisions for yourself, you are said to be "legally incompetent" (also called *incapacitated person* or *mentally incompetent*). Some type of arrangement must be made so that decisions can be made for you. A family member (and not always the one you might choose or the one with your best interest at heart) might petition the court to have you declared incompetent and to name someone to act on your behalf—a *guardian* (although the terminology differs among states). *Conservator, committee,* and other terms might be used. In some states, the term *conservator* refers to a person appointed when you voluntarily seek help, whereas a *guardian* is a person appointed without your consent.

> **Famous Case Study**
> Groucho Marx was disabled by a stroke and hip surgery in 1977. His "companion/manager," Erin Fleming, fought against Groucho's three children to control both Groucho and his assets. When Groucho eventually died, there was an ugly fight over his estate, which lasted for six years. Groucho's three children as well as his three ex-wives ended up receiving almost nothing from his estate. With proper documentation and planning—a guardianship appointment in a health care proxy, a funded revocable living trust, and so on—these issues could have been avoided.

141

Guardians of Persons

A guardian of the person is the type of guardian most people think of when they hear the word *guardian*. A guardian is the individual, or individuals, designated to take care of a minor child or, as in the case of Groucho, an incompetent adult. The guardian of your person may make decisions and assume responsibility for your medical care, nursing care, and related decisions.

Guardians of Property

A guardian can be appointed to protect the interests in an incompetent person's assets. In such cases, the court may establish a guardianship for the property. While similar in concept to a trust, such a guardianship is subject to administration by the court and follows state law. You can arrange a trust, by contrast, while you are competent, with far greater flexibility. The guardian of your property has the job to manage, invest, and distribute your property for your care and benefit.

Guardian Ad Litem

If a minor or incompetent person, in the view of the court, needs protection, the court may appoint a special person to protect and represent the minor or incompetent's interest. This person is referred to as a *guardian ad litem*.

WHEN MIGHT A COURT APPOINT A GUARDIAN FOR YOU?

The court will have to make a determination, based on evidence (e.g., medical records) and testimony of experts (such as your attending physician) and others (family and perhaps unrelated people who know you personally), that you need someone to make decisions for you.

For a person to be subject to a guardianship, it must be demonstrated, in accordance with the provisions of the statute and the applicable court rules, that he or she is a mental incompetent. A *mental incompetent* is defined as a person who is impaired by reason of mental deficiency to the extent that he or she lacks sufficient capacity to govern himself or herself and manage his or her affairs. This can also apply to a person who is impaired as a result of a physical illness or disability. This determination can be made without a jury.

To be classified as a mental incompetent, there must be more than a mere impairment of the mind. However, the incapacity need not be total. This is important since even an incompetent person can have periods of lucidity. The key focus should be whether the individual involved is incapable of governing himself or herself and managing his or her affairs or is unfit for self-control.

DESIGNATE YOUR GUARDIAN IN YOUR HEALTH CARE PROXY

Your state law may have a list, in order of priority, specifying whom a court should consider naming as your guardian. The list might vary by state, but it often starts with your spouse if he or she is living with you, then your heirs, such as your children.

You can designate whom you would want to serve as your guardian, should one ever have to be appointed, in your health care proxy. As noted in Chapter 5, if you have confidence in someone to serve as your health care agent, you should likely trust that same person to serve as your guardian. Few decisions can be more final or significant than those entrusted to your health care agent. You should, thus, likely trust the same person to make decisions if a court has to appoint someone to act on your behalf.

WHAT DOES A GUARDIANSHIP PROCEEDING INVOLVE?

The first step in a guardianship proceeding is for someone to file a petition in court requesting that a guardian be appointed to act for you. The petitioner could be a family member (spouse or next of kin) or other loved one or an institution where you may then be living. You could even petition for yourself in some instances. For example, if you are in the early stages of Alzheimer's and realize that the formalities of a court-appointed guardianship may be safer or preferable to simply letting fate take its course (which might include a court picking your guardian), you might institute the proceeding.

In What Court Does Filing Occur?

The location (venue) for the hearing (an action) for the appointment of a guardian is the county where you were domiciled (permanently residing) at the commencement of the action. This may not be the same county, or even the same state, in which the executor of your will would commence a probate proceeding.

Information Typically Included in the Court Filing

The legal documents filed to begin a guardianship proceeding (complaint) typically include:

1. Name, age, and domicile of the allegedly incompetent person.
2. Name and address of the person bringing the action (the plaintiff), such as a spouse.
3. The relationship of the plaintiff and his or her interest in the action. (For example, if the plaintiff is your nephew, the details would include how the nephew is related to you and why he is concerned about your well-being. Perhaps the nephew has been responsible for your care; perhaps you have lived with the nephew for many years and now a more formal arrangement is necessary.)
4. The name, domicile, and address of spouse, children, and other next of kin. If any of these persons are deceased,

this fact would be noted. The court uses this information to be certain that key people who might be interested in your welfare and who might have information relevant to the proceeding are notified in advance.

5. The name and address of the institution presently providing care. If there is a particular administrator or doctor responsible, his or her name and telephone number are typically included.

6. The period of time during which you have been incompetent and/or under the care of an institution. This should include all relevant details such as the dates, names, and addresses of any institutions; the names and addresses of the primary physicians responsible for your care; and other relevant facts.

7. Formal written statements (affidavits) and exhibits (charts, reports, other information) are typically attached to the complaint providing proof of incompetency and supporting the statements made in the complaint. The allegations in the complaint and the affidavits must be prepared with the formalities required in the statute (verified). Typically, at least two physicians with the qualifications required by the state's statute must submit affidavits as part of the investigation. The affidavits must be made with personal knowledge and may state only facts that the person making the affidavit could testify to, which means that affidavits by physicians must be made by attending physicians who have personally examined you and not by physicians who have merely reviewed your records or reports of others. Neither physician can be a relative of yours. Nor can either physician be a proprietor, director, or chief executive officer of the institution where you are being cared for or financially interested in that institution. This requirement prevents a conflict of interest. If the physician had a financial benefit from your continued care in a certain manner, his or her opinion might be biased. The affidavit should state that the physicians have made personal examinations of you

within a specified number of days of the date of their affidavits. The actual number of days varies by state. The physicians' affidavits must conclude that you are unfit and unable to govern yourself and to manage your own personal and financial affairs. The affidavits should provide in sufficient detail information concerning the circumstances and conduct on which the physicians' conclusions are made. This discussion of your circumstances should include the history of your condition. The affidavits often include specific examples of acts and expressions evidencing that you are of an unsound mind.

8. There must also be an affidavit containing the nature, location, and fair market value of your assets. Amounts of insurance and other assets should be disclosed as well. If this information cannot be obtained, the fact that it cannot be obtained and an explanation should be documented. It is common to attach a photocopy of a recent federal income tax return and copies of any brokerage and bank statements as exhibits to the complaint.

The more detailed, accurate, and complete the complaint and attachments are, the quicker and less costly the next step of the process will likely be.

Court Investigation

Once a document is filed with the court to begin the proceeding (a *petition* or *complaint*), the court will order an independent investigation of your circumstances. Courts are not strangers to abuse by a child, other heir, or even someone not intended to become an heir, who brings a proceeding to take unfair advantage of the person. Heirs will continue to abuse the legal documents and court system to take advantage of those who are helpless; thus, a court often appoints an independent person to investigate the person's status. Your carefully thought-out planning, including a living will, health care proxy, guardianship appointment, as well as the other steps discussed in Chapter 10 will help you avoid such abuse.

After reviewing the documents submitted, if the court determines that a reasonable argument of incompetence exists, the court will require (enter an order) that the court review the matter at some future date (hearing). The court will direct that written communication (notice) be given to you as the alleged incompetent, your family members, and the person responsible for your care. The court will also order the appointment of an attorney, or you can hire an attorney of your own choosing.

Formal Court Hearing

Once the investigation process is completed, there is usually a court hearing before a judge (*magistrate* in some courts) to review testimony, reports, and any relevant facts to make a determination. Before the formal court hearing, state law will likely require formal notice to people who might be interested in the process or your well-being to make sure all relevant views are heard. Most states require affidavits from at least two physicians who have personally examined you within some reasonable time period before the hearing. These may be the same reports used in the investigation, updated to the date of the hearing, or new reports. Generally, but not always, you will be present at this hearing because the court often wants to see for itself your condition and ability. The hearing might be before a judge alone or, in some instances, before a jury (the rules differ by state). If the court concludes that a person should be appointed as a guardian, the court will make the appointment official.

As part of appointing a guardian, the court will have to determine that you are incapable of managing your own affairs. The court may also direct the payment of the physicians, other experts, and attorneys involved. The guardian may be required to have a bond—an arrangement to ensure that the guardian complies with the requirements the court sets. Finally, the guardian must formally accept the appointment. There are many different types of guardianship appointments, and the types vary by state. The guardianship may be a general one with broad authority or more limited. For example, the court may appoint a special medical guardian if there is an emergency health issue and you have not signed a living will or health care proxy and are incompetent to make medical decisions for yourself.

COURT MONITORING YOUR GUARDIAN AFTER APPOINTMENT

The process does not end with the appointment, and it should not. The court will continue to exercise involvement in your case by requiring periodic reports from the guardian and perhaps by exercising other powers of supervision or control over the guardian. The court supervision can be a formality, time drain, nuisance, and cost for some guardians, especially those close to you, who really have your best interests at heart. On the other hand, if someone has selfish motives, such as to benefit from your financial resources when appointed, or worse, simply neglects to take care of you, the court supervision may not be enough. It's really impossible for a system to establish fixed rules (which it must to operate) to deal with the myriad possible situations that might arise.

THINGS YOU SHOULD KNOW WHEN SERVING AS GUARDIAN

Your responsibility as a guardian is to carry out the terms of the court order that appointed you and to comply with state law governing guardianship, as well as specific requirements of the county or court in which you were appointed. You should carefully review the documents involved (court order, etc.) to understand what you must do. There are, however, a host of general responsibilities with which you must be familiar. The best approach is to address these responsibilities at an initial meeting with an attorney representing you as guardian.

Duties You Owe to the Incompetent (Ward)

You owe a duty of loyalty to your ward. You have a duty to administer the assets of your ward (the estate). This means that you must do what is reasonably necessary for the good of the ward's estate and those interested in it (e.g., your ward may have minor children). You must act with care and prudence to protect the ward's estate, invest the ward's assets, and handle matters pertaining to the ward individually (if you are a guardian of the ward's person) and the ward's assets (if you are a guardian of the ward's property). You must always maintain accurate records. You must act to preserve the ward's assets, which can include a host of requirements—from making sure there is adequate fire and casualty insurance, to installing a fence around a swimming pool, to being certain that the money managers you've retained follow a reasonable investment policy.

Authority to Retain Agents

You have a duty to your ward not to delegate to others acts that you can reasonably perform yourself. This does not, however, require you to be an expert in all matters. You can, and often should, hire professionals to perform specialized or expert tasks for which you don't have the training. However, your delegation of a particular act does not absolve you of responsibility to monitor the professionals.

You generally have the power to perform every act that a prudent person would perform for the purposes of fulfilling the directives in the will or trust. This includes the power to employ persons, including attorneys, auditors, investment advisers, or agents, to advise or assist you in the performance of your administrative duties. How far you will be permitted to act without independent investigation upon their recommendations could depend on the facts involved, state law, and the court order appointing you. For example, in some areas the court itself manages your ward's assets and you do not have that responsibility. It is always best to have some level of independent review, entailing at minimum periodic reporting.

Avoid Self-Dealing Issues

As a guardian, you are a fiduciary. This is a position of trust. You cannot violate that trust by engaging in transactions that a trusted and independent person would not consider appropriate. You should not lend money to or borrow money from the ward's estate. Avoid any transaction that could be inappropriate or even appear inappropriate. Self-dealing, such as hiring yourself to perform additional work for additional fees or buying assets from the ward's estate, should be avoided. The risk of self-dealing is present anytime you as guardian employ yourself to perform a service that an independent agent (e.g., a realtor, accountant, or attorney) could also perform.

Your Liability When Serving as a Guardian

Accepting the job of guardian entitles you to earn whatever fees state law permits. However, the position of guardian is not without responsibility, which also brings risks and liabilities, none of which should be taken lightly. If you're cavalier about your tasks, a court could surcharge you personally for expenses or losses if the court finds that you did not act appropriately. While the standard of care for a fiduciary is that of a reasonably prudent person, the court will have the advantage of hindsight in reviewing your actions as guardian. What might have seemed reasonable to you at the time may look inappropriate after the fact. Therefore, you should take steps to minimize the likelihood of being held liable, such as:

1. If there is any conflict of interest between you and the ward, be certain to have the court approve any actions that could be questioned. Better still, try to find an alternative course of action that doesn't involve a conflict of interest.

2. Do you have sufficient experience to handle the matters you are taking care of? If not, hire professionals when a particular task exceeds your experience. Once you've hired a professional, monitor his or her performance. Request periodic reports.

3. Be sure to set up a calendar of key deadlines. These should include deadlines the court advises you of (such as periodic reporting, filing an inventory of your ward's assets, etc.) and deadlines your attorney and accountant advise you of (tax return deadlines, notices to certain persons other than the court, etc.). These could include various deadlines based on the state and court involved. State and federal tax deadlines are critical to meet. Do not assume that every deadline will be monitored by the professionals; you remain responsible to do so as guardian.

4. If there is a major issue, particularly a contentious matter, consult your attorney about the possibility of obtaining a court order specifying the action you should take.

If You Don't Want to Serve as Guardian (Renunciation)

In some instances, it will prove advisable to forgo serving as a guardian. If all the responsibility (see previous discussion of your obligations and potential liability), paperwork, headaches, and so on seem like too much for you (you have inadequate background and experience, your job or other responsibilities are too demanding) or circumstances have changed (you've moved to another state, your relationship with the ward has changed), consider declining the appointment as guardian. You don't have to serve. Remember, it is always simpler, easier, and safer to decline to serve before accepting the position than to resign once appointed.

Example: Two of your brother's three children, your nephews, are heirs under your brother's current will. Your brother named you to serve as guardian in his health care proxy, and a court is willing to confirm that appointment. At the time your brother drafted his health care proxy, his three sons were young and amicable and all named beneficiaries in his will. Your brother never revised your appointment as his guardian. By the time your brother became incompetent, his three children were grown and were feuding. Your brother disinherited one of his three sons. Why insert yourself into the fray among the three nephews? Decline to serve.

Once you have made a decision to decline (or resign after being appointed), be certain that you hire a lawyer to assist you. Forms and reports will have to be filed with the court indicating that you are declining to accept the appointment or resigning after having served. If you've served, you will have the legal responsibility for that time period. You may also need to have a formal financial report prepared for that time period (an accounting) of all monies you had responsibility for as guardian to prove that everything was handled properly. If you never accept the appointment, these issues are avoided.

QUESTIONS TO CONSIDER

About the Guardianship Process and You

1. Would you name the same person as agent under your health care proxy and as guardian of your person? If not, why?

2. Have you planned for your potential disability by preparing a living will, health care proxy with guardianship appointment, and a funded revocable living trust?

3. Will you be better protected by having different people responsible for personal and monetary aspects of your care?

About Your Serving as Someone Else's Guardian

1. Are you comfortable being a guardian?

2. What responsibilities are you likely to have under the circumstances, and are you able to deal with them?

3. What other family members may be interested in what you do? Will they be cooperative?
4. Do you know what responsibilities are inherent in being a guardian?
5. If you don't want to accept the guardianship, what can you do?

CHAPTER SUMMARY

Guardianship is integrally related to your health care and end-of-life decisions and should be considered a part of your overall planning. There are many different types of guardianship, but with respect to your health care proxy, the key issue to address is designating your agent to serve as a guardian of your person (for personal, not monetary, matters). Consider addressing this issue directly in your health care proxy. If not addressed, it is more likely that a court will determine who will be responsible for your personal decisions. This chapter provided an overview of that process and discussed the merits of acting affirmatively to communicate your wishes in advance.

In some instances, you may be asked to serve as a guardian for a loved one. There are many fiduciary responsibilities when serving as a guardian. It is an important position and not one to be taken lightly.

8 SAMPLE ANNOTATED GUARDIANSHIP DESIGNATION FORM

DESIGNATING A PERSON TO ACT AS YOUR GUARDIAN

Since your health care proxy is already appointing a person (and successors if that person cannot act) to make key life and death decisions, this person is probably the same person you would designate to serve as your guardian. Thus, instead of preparing a third document (i.e., in addition to your living will and health care proxy), you can simply add a provision to your health care proxy making the appointment. This decision, however, should be reviewed with an attorney in your state because there may be some benefit of having a third document.

Your health care proxy could provide that, to the extent permitted by law, you wish to designate a person to serve as your guardian. The document should then state that you nominate your health care agent to serve as your guardian. To make your wishes clear to the court, specify that your agent is to serve as a special medical guardian, conservator, or in any similar representative capacity.

You probably should not designate your agent to serve as a guardian of your property because financial powers are better dealt with in your durable power of attorney for financial matters and revocable living trust (see Chapter 10). You might even expressly state in your guardianship designation that your intent in the appointment of a guardian or conservator under your health care proxy is not to revoke or supersede any separate durable power of attorney for financial matters if you have signed one, and that document remains unaffected. This statement should communicate your intent that your separate durable power of attorney for financial matters continue to govern financial matters and the appointment of a conservator or guardian under your health care proxy is solely for the purposes of governing personal, medical, and other such matters.

You can request that any court that may be involved in the appointment of a guardian, special medical guardian, conservator, or similar representative for you at any future date give the greatest weight to your request and designation of a guardian.

Similar to the naming of successor agents under your health care proxy if your primary health care agent cannot serve, you can name your successor health care agents to serve as successor guardians if your primary choice is unable or unwilling to act.

State law will likely require that your guardian post bond (pay a fee to a company to guarantee payment if he violates his duties) to serve in that capacity. To avoid this expense, you can state expressly in the guardianship designation included in your health care proxy that any person appointed as your guardian "shall serve without bond."

GUARDIANSHIP PROCEEDING FORMS

The forms for a guardianship proceeding vary considerably from state to state and vary depending on the facts involved. The following illustrative forms, however, provide a feeling for the formality and issues involved. It is probably never advisable to attempt a guardianship proceeding without the help of an attorney. These documents, therefore, are presented with annotations in this chapter, not as tear-out forms as in a later chapter.

SAMPLE ORDER TO SHOW CAUSE FOR HEARING APPOINTING A GUARDIAN

Lawyer's Name
Lawyer's Address
Lawyer's City, State Zip Code
Lawyer's Telephone Number

IN THE MATTER OF	NAME OF COURT OF STATE COURT DIVISION:
Your Name	COUNTY NAME PROBATE PART DOCKET NO. _____
An Alleged Incapacitated Person	*Civil Action* **ORDER TO SHOW CAUSE FOR HEARING APPOINTING A GUARDIAN OF THE PERSON AND PROPERTY OF _____ [your name]**

1. Upon the reading of the verified complaint and the affidavits and certifications attached to the complaint (the "Documents"), it appears that _____ [your name], an alleged incapacitated person, may be presently unable to manage his [correct gender in all illustrative forms if a female is involved] person and property [this is a full guardianship to cover management of both personal matters and assets] by reason of illness, infirmity, mental weakness, or other cause. Further, it appears from the Documents, the nature of this matter is such that it may be heard and disposed of in a summary manner [without a formal hearing in court] and for good cause otherwise shown:

2. IT IS, on this _____ [month] _____ [day] , of _____ [year]:

3. ORDERED, that _____ [your name], an alleged incapacitated person, and the next-of-kin and parties in interest listed in the Verified complaint show cause before the Honorable _____ [judge's name], in the County of _____ [county name], on the _____ [day] of _____ [month], _____ [year], at the time of _____ [time], or as soon thereafter as counsel can be heard, why an Order should not be entered:

a. Adjudicating [judging or determining that] _____ [your name] to be a person in need of a guardian, as a result of being unable to govern himself and manage his affairs.

b. Granting Letters of Guardianship of the person and property [it might be just one or the other, it doesn't have to be both] of _____ [your name] to _____ [guardian's name] in accordance with the provisions of applicable state law of _____ [state], and on the grounds and basis that _____ [your name] is not able to govern and manage his person and property.

c. Appointing _____ [guardian's name], as medical Guardian of _____ [your name] with the authority to withhold, withdraw, or provide life-sustaining medical treatment; and

d. Granting such other relief as the court may deem just and proper.

4. IT IS FURTHER ORDERED, that _____, [your lawyer's name] Esq. is hereby appointed counsel for _____ [your name], an alleged incapacitated person.

5. IT IS FURTHER ORDERED, that at least _____ (_____) [number of days] days' advance written notice of the hearing be given to _____ [your name], an alleged incapacitated person, and to the alleged incapacitated person's next-of-kin, who include the persons listed in the chart below, and to the alleged incapacitated person's court-appointed attorney _____ .

Name of Relative	Relationship of Relative	Explanation of Relationship	Address, Telephone Number

6. IT IS FURTHER ORDERED, that a copy of the Order to Show Cause for Hearing Appointing a Guardian of the Person and Property of _____ [your name], including the Verified complaint with supporting documents, and Proposed Judgment be served upon [sent to in accordance with any required formalities, such as by certified mail with a return receipt requested]:

a. _____ [your name], personally _____ (_____) [number of days] days before the return date [a formal specific date set by statute].

b. All other interested parties named above by certified mail, return receipt requested, _____ (_____) [number of days] days before the return date.

7. IT IS FURTHER ORDERED, that the Notice of Hearing to _____ [your name] shall contain a statement that if he desires to oppose this action appointing a guardian for him, he may appear in front of the court personally, or by an attorney representing him, and if he so desires, he may obtain a trial by jury.

_____ Signature of Judge

_____ , [judge's name] JSC

SAMPLE VERIFIED COMPLAINT FOR THE APPOINTMENT OF A GUARDIAN FOR AN ALLEGED INCAPACITATED PERSON

[This document illustrates the complaint, which is the key document to begin the guardianship process and make the case for your incapacity to the court.]

Lawyer's Name
Lawyer's Address
Lawyer's City, State Zip Code
Lawyer's Telephone Number

IN THE MATTER OF	SUPERIOR COURT OF NEW JERSEY CHANCERY DIVISION:
Your Name	COUNTY OF _____ PROBATE PART DOCKET NO. _____
An Alleged Incapacitated Person	*Civil Action* **VERIFIED COMPLAINT FOR THE APPOINTMENT OF A GUARDIAN FOR _____ [your name], AN ALLEGED INCAPACITATED PERSON**

Petitioner, _____ [petitioner's name] [person beginning the process of asking the court to rule on your competency and appoint a guardian, such as your spouse] residing at _____ [petitioner's address] (called the "Petitioner"), by way of Verified Complaint, states the following:

1. Petitioner's name is _____ .
2. Petitioner's relationship to _____ [your name], the Alleged Incompetent, is _____ [describe your relationship].
3. The next-of-kin interested in this proceeding are as follows: [List relative names, addresses, and relationships here. In some instances, this is not a simple task for someone with few close relatives or relatives scattered geographically.]

All of the individuals named above are competent, of legal age, and not serving in the military. [Note any exceptions to these criteria. The court may then mandate special steps to ensure that such people receive notice of your guardianship proceeding or appoint someone, such as another guardian, to act on behalf of these people.]

4. [The petitioner's lawyer lists each aspect of the allegations of your incompetence and lists attached exhibits that corroborate the allegations.]

WHEREFORE, Petitioner demands that this court enter Judgment: [After the petitioner has stated and proven the case that you're incompetent, he or she asks the court to rule accordingly and appoint a guardian.]

a. Adjudicating _____ [your name] to be an incapacitated person as defined under applicable state law.

    b. Appointing _____ [guardian's name] as the Guardian of the person of _____ [your name].

    c. Appointing _____ [guardian's name] as the Medical Guardian of _____ [your name], with the authority to consent to any and all medical treatments and procedures necessary for the benefit and physical and mental well-being of _____ [your name]. [Depending on the circumstances and state law, the Guardian of your Person may be vested with all medical decision making, or a separate medical guardian may be appointed.]

    d. Appointing _____ [guardian's name] as the Guardian of the property of _____ [your name]. [The guardian of the property can be the same person or a different person from the guardian of your person.]

    e. Granting such other and further relief as may be just and appropriate for the benefit of _____ [your name].

Petitioner's Lawyer's Name
Petitioner's Lawyer's Firm
Petitioner's Lawyer's Address
Petitioner's Lawyer's Telephone Numbers

Attorney for _____ [guardian's name], Petitioner

By _____ [lawyer's signature]

_____ [lawyer's name]

Dated: _____ [month] _____ [day], _____ [year]

[Some court forms may require that the attorney or the person submitting the form (in this case, the petitioner) who is trying to have you declared incompetent attach specified signed statements to the form (certification). For example, some states may require that a certification be attached stating that it is not anticipated at this time that there is any other party who should be joined in the lawsuit (this "action").]

[Some court forms may require that the attorney or the person submitting the form (in this case, the petitioner) who is trying to have you declared incompetent attach specified signed statements to the form (verification) signed with specific formalities, such as a notary. For example, some states may require that a verification be attached stating that the person to be appointed as guardian is an adult ("being of full age"), believes that the allegations contained in the Verified Complaint are true to the best of his or her knowledge, and so on.]

SAMPLE PHYSICIAN CERTIFICATION

[A statement (certification) signed by your attending physician is a key document in any incompetency proceeding. If someone, such as you, is to challenge the proceeding, the determination of the physician is often the focus.]

Re: _____ [your name]
     An Alleged Incompetent

_____ [physician's name], hereby states as follows:

1. I am a permanent resident of the state of _____ and a physician licensed to practice medicine in the state of _____. I have been licensed to practice in this state for _____ (_____) years. I graduated from the following medical school, _____, in the year _____. I am board certified in _____ [list specialties].

2. I am not a relative either through blood or marriage of the alleged incompetent, _____ [your name].

3. I am not a proprietor, director, or chief executive officer of any institution in which the alleged incompetent, _____ [your name], is living or in which it is proposed to place him or in which he is receiving care currently [modify the details to fit the facts at hand].

4. I am not employed by the management of any of the institutions listed above as a resident physician nor do I have any financial interests in the profits of any of those institutions.

5. I am _____ [your name]'s examining physician.

6. On _____ [month] _____ [day], _____ [year], I personally conducted a physical exam of _____ [your name] at _____ [hospital name], located at _____ [hospital address], in the county of _____ [county name], in the state of _____.

7. The following are the details of that examination:

    a. _____ [your name] is a _____. [The physician should describe your condition in detail.]

    b. Based on my examination of _____ [your name], it is my medical opinion that _____ [your name] has the following medical conditions: [The physician should describe the prognosis in detail.]

    c. As a result of the above prognosis, I conclude that _____ [your name] is unfit and unable to govern his affairs and is therefore mentally incompetent. [The physician should be certain to obtain the legal definition of *incompetent* and expressly address the terminology and criteria in that definition.]

    d. _____ [your name] is not [or is, as the case may be] capable of attending a guardianship hearing due to [reason; e.g., severe dementia and lack of insight into his cognitive dysfunction].

I certify that the foregoing statements are true. I understand that if any of the above statements are willfully false, I am subject to punishment.

_____ [physician's signature]

_____ [physician's name]

[Generally, at least two physician reports are attached.]

SAMPLE ORDER SETTING HEARING DATE FOR APPOINTMENT OF A GUARDIAN

Lawyer's Name
Lawyer's Address
Lawyer's City, State Zip Code
Lawyer's Telephone Number

IN THE MATTER OF	SUPERIOR COURT OF NEW JERSEY
	CHANCERY DIVISION:
Your Name	COUNTY OF _____
	PROBATE PART
	DOCKET NO. _____
An Alleged Incapacitated	
Person	*Civil Action*
	ORDER SETTING HEARING DATE FOR
	APPOINTMENT OF FULL GUARDIAN

1. THIS MATTER having been opened to the court by _____ [plaintiff's attorney's name], attorneys for the Plaintiff, for _____ [plaintiff's name] [insert name of person commencing the action to prove you incompetent, such as your spouse]. The attorney named above is appearing on behalf of the Plaintiff.

2. The court, having read the Verified Complaint and the reports and exhibits attached to it, is satisfied with the legal sufficiency thereof [i.e., the court has concluded that you are possibly incompetent and further steps should be taken] that further proceedings be taken thereon to consider the need to appoint a Full Guardian for _____ [your name].

3. This order is dated on this _____ [day] _____ [month], _____ [year].

4. ORDERED that this matter be set down for a hearing before this court on the _____ [day] _____ [month], _____ [year], at _____ [time], or as soon thereafter as counsel may be heard, in Courtroom Number _____, Floor _____, at _____ [court address], before the Honorable _____ [judge's name].

5. ORDERED that, _____ [court-appointed attorney's name], Esq. is hereby appointed to serve as court-appointed counsel for the alleged incapacitated person, _____ [your name], pursuant to applicable state law of _____ [state]. The court-appointed counsel is to file a written report with the court and serve [deliver] a copy thereof upon the court and upon Petitioner's attorney at least three (3) days prior to the return date [a date set by the court], making recommendations on the application, unless the attorney opposes the application declaring _____ [your name] incompetent.

6. Pursuant to applicable _____ [state] state law, opposition papers [documents disagreeing with the position that you are incompetent] should be submitted to the court no later than five (5) days prior to the hearing. Such report shall also contain a statement as to whether the alleged incapacitated person

desires to be present in Court. The attorney shall have the power to examine records pertaining to the alleged incapacitated person and to visit and confirm with the alleged incapacitated person in order to make his determinations. The attorney is to be compensated out of the estate of _____ [your name], the alleged incapacitated person.

7. ORDERED that pursuant to applicable state law of _____ [state], at least twenty (20) days' notice of such hearing and the Verified Complaint and all pleadings be served personally upon _____ [your name], by _____ [plaintiff's attorney's name]. _____ [court-appointed attorney's name] shall advise _____ [your name] of his right to oppose the action declaring him incompetent, and that he may appear in person or through his attorney. If _____ [your name] desires a trial by jury, he may demand one.

8. ORDERED that pursuant to applicable _____ [state] state law, an Affidavit or Certification of Service and Offer of Assistance [the terminology and procedures vary by state] shall be filed with the court three (3) days prior to the hearing date, that the alleged incapacitated person has been afforded the opportunity to appear personally or by attorney and that he has been given or offered assistance to communicate with friends, relatives, or his attorney.

9. ORDERED that pursuant to applicable state law of _____ [state], that any interested party presently known receive at least thirty-five (35) days' notice, if out of state, and twenty (20) days' notice, if in state, of the court hearing on the Verified Complaint alleging _____ [your name]'s incompetency, and be served with a copy of the Verified Complaint and all pleadings filed in connection with the case, by forwarding them to their last known addresses by certified mail, return receipt requested, within seven (7) days of this Order to the addressees listed on the attached service list.

10. ORDERED that all parties appear and show cause why _____[guardian's name] shall not be appointed full Guardian [This should be consistent with the guardian requests made earlier. If different people are to be named guardian of your person, property, and medical decisions, this statement should clarify that.] for the purpose of maintaining the placement and care of _____ [your name], as well as be granted the power to manage his affairs.

_____ [Judge's Signature]
    Surrogate

QUESTIONS TO CONSIDER

1. Are you fully aware of your responsibilities as well as the pitfalls of being appointed a guardian?
2. Do you understand the ramifications of being appointed guardian? Does it make you reevaluate what measures you might wish to take to avoid this result?
3. Should you designate a guardian in your health care proxy? Should this designation instead be a separate legal form?
4. Should you also have a comprehensive funded revocable living trust to avoid the need for a financial guardian?

CHAPTER SUMMARY

This chapter provided an overview of the forms used in a guardianship proceeding. These forms illustrate the complexity of the process and should encourage you to take actions to avoid having a guardian appointed for you. The forms also illustrate many of the issues and decisions involved in the process if you serve as a guardian.

This chapter also presented a sample guardianship designation form, which states your named guardian, possible alternates, and powers of the guardian.

9 PROTECTING YOUR MINOR CHILDREN

MEDICAL DECISIONS FOR CHILDREN

For those under the age of majority (not a legal adult, as defined in your state's laws), parents or legal guardians (see Chapters 7 and 8) can make medical decisions. While this law is straightforward, common issues do arise that you should address. If you are divorced, the divorce agreement should state which parent is authorized to approve a procedure (or both parents, if applicable). Children over the age of majority should sign their own documents. In most cases, their decisions are relatively simple and are delegated to parents, so simpler and more inexpensive documentation may suffice for them than for adults. Thus, when your children turn 18, they should sign a health care proxy, living will, and power of attorney for financial matters. This leaves one obvious gap: When a child is under the age of majority and both parents are away on a trip, who can authorize medical care for that minor child? Most parents address this issue by writing a letter at the kitchen table the night before the "big trip." It is unlikely that such a hastily written letter will have the necessary information or be as readily accepted as desired. The solution is to prepare and sign an emergency child medical form. This form is based on concepts similar to that of your health care proxy, but tailored to the situation of parents of a minor child on vacation.

This issue may remain a gap in your estate plan concerning your minor children. Guardian appointments under your will take effect only on the death of a parent. Your living will addresses only your health care matters, not those of your minor child. If the parents are on vacation, not reachable, or disabled, who can make a decision concerning a child's medical treatment? In addition, when the child is in the hands of a caregiver and the parents cannot be reached, important personal or medical information may not be known.

AUTHORIZATION FOR EMERGENCY CARE OF MINOR CHILD

You and/or your children's other parent should execute a single, or separate, document stating your name, address, and relationship to each child. The document should declare itself to be your medical authorization, directive, and instruction concerning the care of your child or children.

AGENT OR SURROGATE DECISION MAKER TO AUTHORIZE MEDICAL CARE FOR YOUR MINOR CHILDREN

In case you (or the other parent) are not available in the event of a medical need for your minor child, you should have a signed document in which you authorize and direct that any doctor, hospital, emergency room facility, ambulance, or other medical care provider rely on the instructions of a surrogate decision maker in a medical emergency or until a parent can be contacted.

SURROGATE DECISION MAKER'S INFORMATION

The document should list the initial surrogate and thereafter several alternate surrogates. If any person on your list is not available, the medical care provider should contact the next person and rely on him or her. This should proceed in a manner similar to that described in Chapter 5 concerning your appointing a health care agent for yourself. When listing surrogates, be certain to list on the form all relevant contact information, considering the urgency that might exist. At a minimum, the information should include the surrogate's name, relationship to your child, home address, and all telephone numbers: work, home, vacation, and cellular.

INSURANCE COVERAGE

If you are absent, details about health insurance coverage for your minor child (including, perhaps, a copy of the insurance card) could prove invaluable. List on the form the insurance carrier's name, the name of insured (you, the other parent, etc.), the policy number, group name and number, and contact information.

POWERS AND RIGHTS OF AGENTS

Similar to the form that specifies powers and rights to give to your health care agent (see Chapter 6), the emergency child medical form should give appropriate powers and rights to the surrogate decision makers for your children. These powers, however, should be somewhat limited by the fact that you will likely resume decision making when you become available. In addition, given the young age of the child, it is likely that all measures will be taken to save life (in contrast to the decision process that might occur under a health care proxy for an 80-year-old).

You might authorize the surrogate to make all necessary arrangements for your child at any hospital, emergency room, or other health care facility. The surrogate could be authorized to make any decision reasonably necessary to ensure that all the child's essential needs are provided.

The surrogate might be given the authority to give or withhold consent to any medical procedures, test, or treatment, including surgery; to arrange for the hospitalizations and medical and related care of your child; to summon paramedics or other emergency medical personnel and seek emergency treatment for the child; and to withdraw, modify, or change consent to any medical procedure, test, and treatment, hospitalization convalescent care, home care, or other treatment that you, as the parent of the minor child, may have arranged for the child. Exercise of these powers will be in the context of a young child who, it is hoped, will recover.

To facilitate the surrogate's acting on behalf of your child, you may need to authorize the surrogate to sign, execute, deliver, and acknowledge any contract or other document that may be necessary, desirable, convenient, or proper to exercise any of the powers described in the document.

You may wish to exclude certain matters from the surrogate decision maker's powers, for example, a specific moral or religious belief.

MISCELLANEOUS PROVISIONS

- *No time limit:* You might wish to expressly state that there is no time limit on the effectiveness of the surrogate document. Alternatively, you could state that the document is effective until the child attains the age of 18.

- *Authorization and direction binding:* Your document should state that you (and the other parent) expect all family, physicians, and all those concerned with the care of your child to act as if they are bound to act in accordance with the directions contained in your document.

- *Third parties:* To encourage others to rely on the instructions of the surrogate decision maker on behalf of your child, your document could state that third parties, including but not limited to medical professionals, insurance companies, hospitals, convalescent facilities, or the like, may rely on the representations of the named surrogate as to all matters.

- *Construction:* The document should include the usual standard legal matters such as the state law that governs and other formalities. Both parents should sign the document, and their signatures should be notarized.

MEDICAL HISTORY AND RELATED INFORMATION

Since the person named as surrogate decision maker may not have all the firsthand knowledge necessary to help your child, consider attaching an addendum with important medical information, including:

- Name, address, birth date, and Social Security number for the child.
- Relevant medical information such as blood type, allergies, existing medical conditions, medications taken, child's past medical history, and smoking, drinking, and drug use information.
- General family medical history, especially hereditary conditions that could affect the child.
- Any religious restrictions on the child's care.
- The child's social history, depending on the medical issue.
- If the child is very young, tips on how to comfort the child (favorite toys, etc.) in your absence during a medical emergency.

QUESTIONS TO CONSIDER

1. When you go on vacation, with whom do you leave your children? Are these the same people you would rely on to make emergency medical decisions?
2. Are the people you wish to authorize to make medical decisions on your children's behalf available in the event of an emergency?

3. Have you discussed these issues with your child's pediatrician?

4. Do the caretakers or others know your children's medical history so they can make an informed decision?

CHAPTER SUMMARY

Executing an emergency medical form for benefit of your minor child could be extremely important, even if it is a new concept that hasn't been formally approved by law or court. This step gives decision-making power to a designated person, a surrogate or agent, if your spouse or you are unreachable or unable to make the decisions. Even if you have executed a living will or a health care proxy for yourself, you may not have addressed the needs of your children. If there are specific conditions or circumstances in your family that you need to address, integrate those issues into the planning process.

10 ADDITIONAL STEPS TO PROTECT YOURSELF AND YOUR LOVED ONES

LIVING WILLS AND HEALTH CARE PROXIES ARE ONLY A SMALL PART OF AN OVERALL PLAN TO PROTECT YOURSELF

Your objective should be to protect your dignity, end-of-life decisions, general health care decisions, and all related matters. To achieve this objective, you need to do more than the three steps outlined in previous chapters. The additional recommended steps focus on financial matters that are ancillary but are still important to ensuring your protection (including avoiding a guardianship).

DURABLE POWER OF ATTORNEY FOR FINANCIAL MATTERS

A financial power of attorney is a vital personal planning document. It is a contract in which you grant another person, often your spouse, the power to handle financial and legal matters on your financial behalf in the event you are ill, injured, or unavailable for any reason. The person you grant this authority to is your attorney-in-fact, or agent. Your agent is given the important responsibility of seeing to your financial matters if an emergency prevents your taking the necessary actions.

If you're disabled, a power of attorney can authorize your agent to make gifts and take other actions to minimize your estate and other taxes. Your power of attorney can authorize your financial agent to spend your money to care for your loved ones. Because of an aging population, Medicaid or elder law planning is increasingly common. If you become disabled before implementation of the planning, a durable power (accomplished through a broad gift power in your financial power of attorney) is essential to facilitate the transfer of assets. If you become incapacitated and there is no express gift power in your power of attorney, the gifts won't be recognized.

Relationship of Your Financial Power of Attorney and Your Health Care Proxy

Although the terminology of your financial power of attorney is similar to that of a health care proxy (also called a *health care power of attorney*), the context is very different. Your health care agent should address health care and medical issues. Your financial agent under your financial power of attorney is vested with the power to handle financial, not health care, matters. While there is clearly overlap (your financial agent may pay for health care costs), the powers are clearly independent, and the documents should be kept independent.

Relationship of Your Financial Power of Attorney and Your Revocable Living Trust

A revocable living trust is a contract that creates an arrangement to manage your assets. The revocable trust is not a substitute for a power of attorney because the power of attorney is necessary to handle assets that are not in your trust or legal issues outside the purview of your trustee. You should consider both documents. Even if you have a living trust, you should prepare and sign powers of attorney. Your living trust will cover only the assets you took the necessary legal steps to transfer to it. A power of attorney, however, if broadly written, can give your agent access to all of your nontrust assets. A durable power of attorney immediately terminates on your death, so it can never be considered a substitute for a will or trust arrangement.

Use of a revocable living trust and, in particular, how it can help ensure that your end-of-life decisions are respected are discussed later in this chapter.

Types of Powers of Attorney

A *durable* power of attorney remains effective even though you are disabled. Any financial power of attorney you intend to include with your end-of-life planning should be a durable power of attorney. Generally, you need only this type of power, and you should include in your power of attorney a provision expressly stating that the power of attorney will remain valid even if you become disabled. One of the most important reasons to have a financial power of attorney is to manage assets after you are disabled.

A *springing* power of attorney is one that springs into being (becomes effective) only when you become disabled. This prevents your agent from having any authority until you are actually disabled and need assistance. The drawback to using a springing power of attorney is that your agent will have to prove you've become disabled, which can sometimes present problems, additional work, or delays for the agent. People often use a springing power because they don't feel comfortable granting such power to the person they are naming as agent. You should not grant any power of attorney unless you trust the person named. If trust is not an issue, why risk restricting the power of attorney until you become disabled? If you are setting up a revocable living trust to hold most of your assets, the decision process for your power of attorney may change. If most assets are in your trust, you might feel more comfortable naming an agent whose power is effective immediately (i.e., when you sign the document) rather than springing into effect later.

Comment: The rules differ from state to state. Be certain to consult with an attorney in your state for specific rules that apply to you. For example, some states limit to certain close relatives the people you may name as an attorney-in-fact. In some states, it may be advisable to file (record) the power of attorney in the appropriate governmental office.

Most powers of attorney are *general* powers, which means they include a broad range of provisions to address almost any imaginable situation. In some cases, however, you may want a *special* power of attorney—a power of attorney limited to a few specified uses. For example, you may wish to grant a limited power of attorney to a close colleague to authorize him or her to perform certain functions relating to your business during a period when you are ill or otherwise unavailable. A business power of attorney may even provide for compensation. A business power of attorney should be considered an important planning component for every closely held business.

Standard or *form* powers of attorney use a recognized statutory (state law) form. Some state laws prescribe a particular form of power of attorney. These laws may state that banks must accept a form prepared in accordance with the law. In these cases, you should sign a customized power of attorney form prepared by your attorney because it can offer additional provisions and flexibility that the preprinted standard forms can't. For example, the attorney-prepared power may have a direction to your financial agent to abide by and finance the health care decisions made by your health care agent. You should also sign a power of attorney on the preprinted form because it will be more readily accepted in some instances.

Terms to Include in Your Power of Attorney

You should name one or more alternate agents as a precaution in the event that the primary agent (e.g., your partner or spouse) is unable or unwilling to take the necessary actions. Give careful consideration to the persons named. If there are two financial co-agents, both will have to sign to take any action. In contrast to health care agents, who should not be named as joint agents, you can name co-financial agents.

Your financial power could place restrictions on the scope of the agent's actions. For example, you may permit the payment of only certain emergency expenses; you may permit or not permit the sale of assets, making gifts, and so on. The power should, in detail, authorize your agent to deal with the IRS on a broad range of tax matters and include the right to transfer assets to your revocable living trust.

USE A REVOCABLE LIVING TRUST TO COMPLEMENT YOUR FINANCIAL POWER OF ATTORNEY AND HEALTH CARE PROXY

A revocable inter vivos trust (sometime called a *living trust* or *loving trust*) is one of the most talked about estate planning techniques. While it can be a very useful financial and estate planning tool, much of the talk is hype. Living trusts in the appropriate circumstances can be an ideal tool to accomplish many essential planning goals. A living trust is set up during your lifetime. You retain complete control over the assets in the trust while you are alive and prior to your becoming disabled. If you become disabled or infirm, a successor trustee takes over managing your assets (although it can be preferable to have that successor trustee serve as a co-trustee before you become disabled to facilitate the transition). The key benefit of the revocable living trust to planning for end-of-life and related matters is that if you cannot handle your financial matters, a properly structured revocable living trust will ensure that they are handled for you.

An important part of the disability provisions of your living trust is detailed instructions as to how you should be cared for in the event of disability. Many of the form trusts simply do not provide this type of personalized detail. Do you want to avoid being placed in a nursing home as long as possible? Do you have preferences for the type of health care facility you should be placed in if it becomes absolutely necessary? If geographic preferences are important to you during your life, you should specify in your living trust that in the event of your disability, you wish to be placed in a facility located in a certain part of the country (perhaps near your family). If religious preferences are important, you may wish to specify that the health care facility be near a church, mosque, or synagogue so that you could attend services or that the facility meet your religious dietary requirements. Do not assume that your trustees "will know." Specifying such details may be vital depending on who the trustees are. This detail can also enable your trustees to respond to a challenge by your heirs as to the appropriateness of the decisions and expenditures they make.

Example: You're a 78-year-old widower and have few family other than your children and minor grandchildren. They all live several hundred miles away. A living trust is likely to make sense unless the other facts and circumstances are very persuasive against using such a trust. Considering the ages and scarcity of those who can help in a financial emergency, the use of a living trust may be ideal to provide protection against disability. If you have no fully trusted people to name as successor trustees, you could name an institution to serve as a co-trustee with friends or family members. The institution is subject to substantial regulatory scrutiny and safeguards and thus gives comfort that your assets will be looked after for your benefit. Institutions do not generally serve as agents under a durable power of attorney, so a living trust may be necessary.

A trust is a contract; thus you must have the comprehension, understanding, and state of mind required to create a binding legal contract. The standard for signing a will has intentionally been made easier by law to enable people in extremis to sign wills. The standard merely requires you to be aware of your descendants, the extent of your assets, and the fact that you are signing a document to bequeath those assets to the persons you name. If you are disabled or infirm, you may be legally incapable of signing a contract, but still have sufficient capacity to sign a will. A will, not a living trust, should be used in this case. This scenario illustrates the importance of completing your revocable living trust and other end-of-life planning in advance.

LETTER OF INSTRUCTION

It is essential to communicate your personal desires and objectives to family, friends, and loved ones. Many of these decisions are too personal, variable, or simply inappropriate for inclusion in your legal documents, or they cannot be enforced legally so you will be relying on the respect of loved ones to carry them out. Some of these decisions are too vague to reduce to clear legal terms. Finally, as these personal decisions change over time, a nonbinding informal letter can be revised by you anytime at no cost. This might enable you to avoid the expense of revising expensive legal documents (but check with your advisers).

Suggestion: Your notes and scribbles in this book, unconstrained by the legal formalities that apply to documents such as a living will and health care proxy, can provide insight, a personal touch, and feeling, which no legal document can (or should) capture. Many (most?) people find it difficult, if not impossible, to write a heartfelt letter explaining their wishes to their family, which is an important step. Staring at a blank piece of paper or computer screen while trying to write is really tough for most people. It's even more difficult when the topic you're having to write about is your own demise. Scribbling in this book is much easier. You can simply note your reactions as you read. When you're done, you can then flip through the comments in this book and use those as the starting point for your letter of instruction. If you can't move from notations to a letter, you'll still have left your family tremendous insights.

An essential step in implementing your end-of-life and related planning is preparing a letter of last instruction (the "two tissue box letter") to your loved ones, heirs, and others. Your instructions as to how personal decisions should be made (health care, burial, services, financial, distribution of jewelry and other items, and anything else important to you and your heirs) should be addressed.

There are often a host of personal issues that your agents, family, and others need to know. A personal letter can provide valuable guidance, avoid fights, and help ensure that your goals are carried out.

This letter is likely to be the most difficult step in your entire estate plan. Don't hold up completing all of your documents and planning if you have difficulty writing this letter. Try discussing the least difficult things first. You can always revise the letter later to address some of the tougher issues.

Some personal comments and requests don't belong in formal legal documents. For example, you might select your mother instead of your husband as your health care agent because your marriage is so new. You might select a younger child before an older child. To avoid hurt feelings and the resulting arguments, you might wish to explain the reasoning in a personal note.

Funeral and burial instructions can be described in this letter. Be consistent with what you've included in your living will or will. Including these items in a letter of instruction can be important since a will is often not available in time to make known this information. For example, you might wish to describe in detail some of your personal preferences. Who should eulogize you, in what order? Perhaps there are specific messages you wish to relay. You'd like a wreath of your special flowers. These personal items might be important to you but inappropriate to include in a formal legal document.

If you have minor children, some guidance to a prospective guardian as to the care and raising of your children should be included. This guidance will be so helpful that you should push yourself to get through the pain of writing such a letter.

A copy of your letter can be kept in your safe deposit box, a copy given to your executor, and a copy kept with your original will (which your attorney typically keeps). Because of the highly personal nature of this letter, a form would really not be of much help. Take the time to address the issues important to you. The following is a sample letter of instruction:

Dan Jones
345 West Boulevard
Some Town, Any State

December 12, 2004
Jane Smith
123 Main Avenue
Any Town, Some State

RE: *Letter of Instruction*

Dear Friends and Family:

This letter addresses a number of important personal issues relating to my health care decisions, funeral, and other arrangements. This letter is not legally binding, but it is my hope that you will be morally bound to carry out its instructions. I have written this letter to help you understand and implement the wishes that I have expressed in my health care proxy and living will.

I did not name my beloved wife Cindy as an agent. After many discussions with her, it was clear to me that the burdens of making difficult health care decisions and, in particular, to authorize a DNR for me would be too painful. She was fully aware and agreeable to my instead naming our children as agents. I have noted these decisions here, in this letter, to prevent anyone from speculating or inferring any negative meaning to this decision. My not naming Cindy has not been done because of a lack of love and respect for her, but because of my great love, respect, and caring for her.

I have named the persons listed in my health care proxy and living will to serve as my agents because of my love, respect, and trust in them. I am grateful for each agreeing to serve in that capacity. I have named my younger daughter, Jane Smith, as an agent prior to my son, Steven Jones, not for lack of love or trust in Steven, but because of Jane's geographic proximity to me and medical background. I believe that these attributes enable her to more readily address these issues.

My living will states that in the event of a persistent vegetative state, terminal illness, extreme pain, or other extreme situation where it is obvious that I will have no meaningful quality of life, no heroic measures should be taken. I recognize that these terms are vague. I have spoken at length with my wife and children about my feelings and believe they understand my wishes. I recognize that the statements in my living will may offend the religious views of some family members. It is not my intent to offend or hurt anyone. However, if in the opinion of my attending physicians, there is no meaningful hope of ever having a quality of life, and especially if my continued "life" only serves to cause pain to my family and prevent them from achieving closure for my life, which has for all practical purposes ended, then I want no heroic measures taken to preserve that "life."

In my living will, I was intentionally vague about funeral and burial arrangements because I truly believe that these rights of passage are more for the benefit of the living than the deceased. Therefore, I want to give my family and loved ones the opportunity and, in fact, the encouragement, to select the services, rituals, and burial that would give them the most solace. I would expect that in light of the diverse array of religious and personal beliefs in the family, my family would select a nonsectarian service that would be consoling, but not offensive, to all. I would prefer that no music or open coffin be used as these seem to diminish the solemn nature of the service. However, I reiterate that my family and loved ones should select what will give them the most solace.

I love you all.

Sincerely,

_____

Dan Jones

QUESTIONS TO CONSIDER

1. Have you identified your personal estate planning goals? Do you have the documents to address them?

2. Do you have a durable power of attorney for financial matters? Will your financial agent support, and not undermine, the decisions of your health care agent?

3. Do you have sufficient trustworthy and astute people to rely on for financial, legal, and other important steps?

4. Do you have a revocable living trust? Should you? Is it funded (i.e., have assets been transferred to it)?

5. What issues should you address in a letter of instruction? Are there any issues that people may fight over that you can resolve through a personal note?

CHAPTER SUMMARY

This chapter provided a review of some of the many financial and legal considerations that must be addressed as part of your overall health care and related estate planning. Protecting your end-of-life decisions requires more than just addressing the more obvious health-related documents.

11 HOW TO SIGN YOUR DOCUMENTS AS A STOPGAP BEFORE SEEING A LAWYER

HOW TO USE THE SAMPLE TEAR-OUT FORMS

Sample tear-out forms should be used for purposes of helping you make decisions for your lawyer to incorporate into final forms you rely on. No sample form can substitute for the judgment of years of legal experience.

Before using the illustrative forms, first read, review, and understand the relevant discussions in the prior chapters of this book. The forms should be looked at only after you've studied this book, understand what is involved, made the many personal decisions necessary, and collected the information the forms ask you for. You might wish to make draft copies of the tear-out forms first so that you have a clean set for final use. Then follow these steps:

1. When you've prepared the information to fill in the blanks, the best approach is to type the information in using an electronic version of the forms.

Planning Point: Consult the web site www.healthcareinstructions .com for information on updates, electronic versions of the forms, and other planning ideas. If a pass code is required to access the forms, use the following: LIVWILL2003.

Or, print neatly in pencil on photocopies of the tear-out forms. Use pencil so it is easy to make corrections.

2. Don't sign forms completed in pencil; make photocopies of the forms. The photocopy process converts the pencil markings into ink. It may be best to photocopy the typed-in form as well so you have a clean form for signing.

3. Review the form for blanks. Line out any inappropriate, inapplicable, or blank items. Do not leave any unused blanks in any form you sign.

4. Never write anything below your signature line. It won't be legally binding.

5. For any items you do not want in the form, cross out the inappropriate lines and when you sign the photocopy of the form, initial each sentence or section that was crossed out. If you make any cross-outs on your will, in addition to initialing the photocopy of each page, sentence, or section that was crossed out, each of your witnesses and your notary should initial them as well.

6. When the form you are to sign is completed and copied, staple the form at the top left corner. Never remove the staple from the form because it will appear that the document has been tampered with.

7. Arrange to have two witnesses and a notary with you when you sign your living will and health care proxy (or other document). None of the witnesses or notary should be people that you have named in the documents. It is preferable to have people who live in the area, are over 21, but are reasonably young so they are likely to be available if a question arises in the future. Make arrangements with all involved before the scheduled time of signing. The preferable approach is to hire a lawyer to supervise the signing.

Comment: Before you sign any forms, *stop and think*. Do you really feel confident that you evaluated all the matters discussed in this book? Do you have any unusual, difficult, complex, or risky situations that would make signing forms on your own inappropriate? Do any of the situations for which this book recommends that you seek professional guidance apply to you? Having reached this point of the process, you are an educated consumer, have gathered all relevant data, and will be able to save legal fees ordinarily charged for this kind of work. Think carefully, however, because no single book can substitute for 10, 15, or more years of an estate planner's legal experience. Is there something you're missing? Are there changes in the laws since this book was written that could affect you? Does your state have unique considerations that an attorney in your state should help you address? Before you sign, make sure that this is really the way to go. Backing away from completing your own legal forms may just be the smartest thing you can do to protect yourself and your loved ones.

WHAT TO DO WITH THE FORMS YOU SIGN

Be sure all documents are kept in a safe and secure but accessible location. Give at least one original living will and health care proxy to the agent you named. If the first agent is your spouse, partner, or someone living with you, give a second original to someone named as a successor agent (i.e., who serves if the first agent cannot) to keep outside your home. You can sign several originals. Give your doctor a copy to include in your medical records. (If you want to do it right, next time you have an appointment with your doctor, ask in advance if the doctor can discuss the form with you.) A copy should be kept on top of the refrigerator in your home or somewhere it is easily and quickly available in the event of an emergency.

STEPS TO TAKE TO SIGN YOUR DOCUMENTS

1. Verify in advance which documents are to be signed and be certain they are all prepared with sufficient copies to sign. For living wills and health care proxies, signing three forms for each as originals might be advisable. Keep one at home in a readily accessible location, one with an agent, and consider leaving the third with a successor agent or other trusted person who is likely to be available in an emergency.

2. Every document you plan to sign should be reviewed to be certain that each page is properly accounted for. If any page is missing or somehow not properly copied on the printer or photocopy machine, the deficient document should be redone.

3. Be certain that the correct signing date appears on all documents.

4. Explain to the two witnesses and notary what all documents are, what they do, and why you wish to sign them. Explain the purpose of the documents in one or two brief, simple sentences. Be certain in your explanations to mention enough specifics so it is clear to all the people present that you are familiar with what is in the form, you know the names and relationships of your family members and all people mentioned in the form, you understand the nature of your decisions, and you are generally of sound mind. For example, you might explain:

   My living will and health care proxy provide for decision making in the event medical decisions must be made for my care and I am unable to do so. A living will specifies my feelings concerning life support and other important personal issues. For example, I would wish that if I am in a persistent vegetative state, no heroic measures be taken to prolong my life. However, I don't view the providing of nutrition and hydration as heroic. I also intend to sign a health care proxy, which is a durable power of attorney for health care matters. This designates an agent and provides that agent with a broad range of powers from hiring and firing medical care personnel, to making funeral arrangements, hospice care, and so forth.

5. After you have explained each document, sign all copies. Witnesses and the notary sign where indicated on the documents, and the correct date is placed by the notary signatures. Be sure that the correct state and county are listed where appropriate.

6. You could have the notary ask you the following questions during the signing process, and the answers could be documented to help confirm your competency to sign:
   a. Please state your name.
   b. What is today's date?
   c. Please identify the document in front of you.

Note: In response, you should clearly identify the document placed in front of you as either a living will or a health care proxy.

---

   d. Have you read and reviewed this document?
   e. Do you understand to your satisfaction this document?
   f. Please state the name and relationship of your immediate family members and other persons who are named in your documents as agents.
7. Be sure a photocopy of this checklist is completed for each person who signed documents.

CHAPTER SUMMARY

This chapter provides guidance on using the tear-out forms in the succeeding chapters to implement your health care wishes. The formalities of signing documents is a hurdle that you must evaluate in deciding whether you should endeavor to sign legal documents, such as a living will and health care proxy, on your own.

APPENDIX

Forms

TEAR-OUT LIVING WILL POCKET CARD

LIVING WILL/HEALTH CARE PROXY INFORMATION:

[ ] I have executed a Living Will

[ ] I have executed a Health Care Proxy and appointed:

_____
Name of Agent

(day) _____ (night) _____
Telephone Numbers for Agent

_____
Name of Alternate Agent

(day) _____ (night) _____
Telephone Numbers for Alternate Agent

My Agent has a copy of my Health Care Proxy
[ ] Yes   [ ] No

My Alternate Agent has a copy of my Health Care Proxy
[ ] Yes   [ ] No

_____   _____
Date   My Printed Name

_____
Signature

My [ ] Living Will and/or [ ] Health Care Proxy
can be found:

_____
Location of Living Will and/or Health Care Proxy

Other copies can be found with:

_____
(Name)   (Telephone No.)

_____
(Name)   (Telephone No.)

TEAR-OUT LIVING WILL

LIVING WILL

I, _____ [your name], residing at _____ [your address], being an adult and of sound mind, and being competent and otherwise capable of making the decisions set forth in this Living Will, and having the fundamental right to make voluntary, informed choices to accept, reject, or choose among alternative courses of medical and surgical treatment to the extent permitted in accordance with the standards described below, make this declaration as a directive to be followed if for any reason I become incapacitated or incompetent and thus unable to participate in decisions regarding my medical care. This statement shall stand as an expression of my wishes, beliefs, objectives, and directions (my "Wishes"). It is my specific intent that my Wishes, as stated herein, constitute clear and convincing evidence of such Wishes.

  1. *Recitals.*
        a. **WHEREFORE,** I direct that this Living Will become a part of my permanent medical records.
        b. **WHEREFORE,** I recognize that a time may come when I cannot participate in my medical care decisions, even if there are favorable prospects for my eventual recovery. I know that it is not possible for me to anticipate the diverse medical decisions that may have to be made in the future and give specific written directions at this time. Accordingly, I have executed this Living Will (and a separate Health Care Proxy) appointing an agent, or alternate agent, to make such specific decisions when necessary, and in accordance with my Wishes.
        c. **WHEREFORE,** I wish to direct the actions of my family, friends, clergymen, physicians, nurses, and all those concerned with my care, as provided in this declaration.
        d. **WHEREFORE,** I hereby express my hope that my Wishes be honored by health care facilities and physicians without having to go through the process of any judicial or other determination.
        e. **WHEREFORE,** _____
_____ [fill in any key religious directives].
   NOW THEREFORE, I declare my Wishes to be as follows:

[If you have a nonmarried partner you are naming as agent, modify the following paragraph; otherwise delete it.]

  2. *Visitation by Partner.*
   For purposes of visitation in hospitals, nursing homes, or other facilities, it is my express intent that _____ [partner's name] be treated and considered for all purposes as an immediate family member, and be given the widest latitude and accommodation as if a member of my immediate family and if the Agent named is not a member of my immediate family that such Agent be given

preference over any blood relatives for visitation and other purposes. Under no circumstances should an Agent named herein be denied access for visitation or other purposes because such Agent is not a blood relative.

3.   *Appointment of Attorney-in-Fact and Agent.*

a.   I hereby make, constitute, and appoint ("Grant") _____ [name of first agent], residing at _____ [address of first agent], as my true and lawful Attorney-in-Fact and Health Care Agent for me and in my name, place, and stead and for my benefit, or any alternate appointed in accordance with the provisions of this document (the "Agent").

Telephone Numbers:

Work/Day:

Evening/Home:

Cell:

Pager:

---

4.   *Appointment of Alternate Attorney-in-Fact and Health Care Agent.*

a.   If _____ [name of first agent] is unwilling or unable to act as my Agent, I appoint the first person on the following list who is able and willing to serve as my Alternate Agent:

(1)   _____ [name of second agent], who resides at _____ [address of second agent].

Telephone Numbers:

Work/Day:

Evening/Home:

Cell:

Pager:

---

(2) _____ [name of third agent], who resides at _____ [address of third agent].

Telephone Numbers:

Work/Day:

Evening/Home:

Cell:

Pager:

I request, but do not require, that any Agent appointed above endeavor to consult with _____ [name persons your agent should discuss decisions with], where feasible, prior to taking any action.

b.   Any reference to Agent shall include the Alternate Agent where such Alternate Agent is acting as provided under this Living Will.

c.   If all of the above Agents have predeceased me or are unable or unwilling for any reason to serve as my Agent, but an agent is required by law solely in order to direct the withholding or withdrawal of life-sustaining treatment, or other medical or health care objectives, in accordance with my Wishes, I authorize my attending physician to appoint such an Agent upon consultation with one or more of my relatives, religious advisers (if any are specified herein), friends, or other persons or agencies reasonably believed to be interested in my well-being.

[Delete the provisions that do not reflect your medical wishes, and modify those that remain so that they best reflect your wishes. If there are any religious issues that must be reflected, revisions may be necessary.]

5.   *No Heroic Medical Efforts.*
    a.   *General "No Heroic Measures" Language.*
        (1)   If:
            (a)   I: (i) have an incurable or irreversible, severe mental or severe physical condition; or (ii) am in a state of permanent unconsciousness or profound dementia; or (iii) am severely injured; or (iv) have a terminal illness. For purposes of the above, "terminal illness" shall be defined as an irreversible, incurable, and untreatable condition caused by disease, illness, or injury when an attending physician can certify in writing that, to a reasonable degree of medical certainty, there is no hope of my recovery or death is likely to occur in a brief period of time if life-sustaining treatment is not provided. "Permanently

unconscious" is defined as a state that, to a reasonable degree of medical certainty, an attending physician certifies in writing that I am irreversibly unaware of myself and my environment and there is a total loss of cerebral cortical functioning resulting in my having no capacity to experience pain.

and

(b)   In any of these cases there is no reasonable expectation of recovering from such severe, permanent condition, and regaining any meaningful quality of life, then in any such event, it is my desire and intent that heroic life-sustaining procedures and extraordinary maintenance or medical treatment be withheld and withdrawn.

(2)   Quality of life is of tremendous importance in determining the scope and extent of health care services that I wish. Maintaining my life as a mere biological existence, in a vegetative state, is not an acceptable goal of my medical treatment. Therefore, if there is no reasonable probability (i.e., negligible probability) that any particular medical treatment would benefit me by returning me to a level of functioning or existence where I could communicate with my loved ones, and reasonably understand such communication, I direct that medical treatments, as described herein, be withheld and withdrawn.

(3)   It is not my desire to prolong my life through mechanical means where my body is no longer able to perform vital bodily functions on its own, and where there is little likelihood of ever regaining any meaningful quality of life. The condition and degree of severity and permanence contemplated by this provision are of such a nature and degree of permanent illness, injury, disability, or accompanied by pain such that the average person might contemplate the decisions addressed herein (regardless of whether such person would make the decisions I have made herein).

(4)   In any such event, I direct all physicians and medical facilities in whose care I may be, and my family and all those concerned with my care, to refrain from and cease extraordinary or heroic life-sustaining procedures and artificial maintenance and/or medical treatment. The procedures and treatment to be withheld and withdrawn (i.e., to be considered heroic) include, without limitation, surgery, antibiotics, cardiac and pulmonary resuscitation, ventilation, intubation or other respiratory support (except as provided otherwise under the provision below "Nutrition and Hydration"), medical and surgical tests and treatments and medications diagnostic tests of any nature, and surgical procedures of any nature.

6.   *Nutrition and Hydration.*

[Select a provision that best reflects your wishes and delete the remaining provisions. Revise as necessary.]

a.   *Withhold Nutrition and Hydration Where Attending Physician Certifies.*
If any attending physician shall state in writing to my Agent that I am, to a reasonable degree of medical certainty, in a terminal condition or a permanently unconscious state, and that the provision (or continued provision) of nutrition and

hydration will not, to a reasonable degree of medical certainty, prolong my life in accordance with my Wishes, provide comfort to me, or minimize my pain or discomfort, then my Agent shall authorize and direct the provision of further nutrition or hydration.

     b. *Withhold Nutrition and Hydration Only in Accordance with Standards for Withholding Medical Care Generally.*

Any artificially administered nutrition and hydration (feeding and fluids) are to be considered as extraordinary and heroic measures and as such they may be withheld and withdrawn when other life-sustaining treatments are withheld or withdrawn in accordance with the standards set forth in the preceding paragraphs. In the event that this provision is contrary to applicable state law, I request that my requests be honored to the extent so permitted.

For purposes of this provision, nutrition and hydration shall include, by way of example, and not limitation, tube feedings, Corpak tubes, nasogastric tubes, Levin tubes, gastrostomy tube, or hyperalimentation.

     c. *Withhold Nutrition and Hydration If a Physician Certifies That There Is Loss of Cognition.*

If any attending physician shall certify in writing to my Agent that, to a reasonable degree of medical certainty, I have experienced a neurologically determined loss of cognition and communication which I am unlikely to recover, then nutrition and hydration may be withheld and withdrawn. In the event that this provision is contrary to applicable state law, I request that my requests be honored to the extent so permitted.

     d. *Do Not Withhold Nutrition or Hydration.*

Artificially administered nutrition and hydration (feeding and fluids) may not be withheld, and I specifically request that they be administered when medically appropriate.

I AGREE TO ABOVE NUTRITION/HYDRATION PROVISION:

_____ [Your signature]

---

7. *Medication and Treatments to Alleviate Pain and Suffering.*

[Select a provision that best reflects your wishes and delete the remaining provisions. Revise as necessary.]

     a. *Provide Maximum Pain Relief.*

Even if procedures and treatments are to be withheld or withdrawn, I wish that all palliative treatment and measures for my comfort, and to alleviate my pain, be continued. Such efforts to relieve pain may be continued even if such measures may: shorten my life, lead to permanent addiction, have potentially dangerous ancillary consequences, render me unconscious, or lead to permanent physical damage.

   b.   *Provide Pain Relief but Do Not Intentionally Hasten Death.*

Even if procedures and treatments are to be withheld or withdrawn, I wish that all palliative treatment and measures for my comfort, and to alleviate my pain, be continued. Pain relief may be continued even if as an unintended result of such measures my life span is shortened. However, pain relief should not affirmatively be used as a means of intentionally hastening my death.

   8.   *Pregnancy.*

[Select a provision that best reflects your wishes and delete the remaining provisions. Revise as necessary.]

   a.   *Preference to My Life over the Life of My Fetus.*

In the event that I am pregnant, I direct that preference be given to me over the life of my fetus in any decisions that must be made and that I receive primary consideration over my fetus in any decision-making process.

   b.   *Endeavor to Save My Child Where the Child May Have Reasonable Quality of Life.*

In the event that I am pregnant, I direct that all life-sustaining treatment be continued during the course of my pregnancy where there is reasonable hope of my child being born healthy and able to lead a normal life, and that my fetus receive primary consideration over me in any decision-making process.

   9.   *Wishes Concerning Living Arrangements.*

[Modify the following to reflect your wishes.]

It is my wish that I live my last days at home rather than in a hospital if such an arrangement would not jeopardize the chance of a meaningful recovery, impose undue burden on my family, or prevent my obtaining maximum pain relief for any illness from which I suffer.

   10.   *Transfer or Removal to Another Health Care Facility.*

In the event that any health care facility in which I am located is unwilling or unable to carry out my Wishes, I authorize my Agent, in my Agent's absolute discretion, to have me moved to another health care facility which, in my Agent's reasonable expectation, may be able and willing to carry out my Wishes. I direct that my health care providers cooperate with, and assist, my Agent in promptly transferring me to another health care facility. I further direct my medical care provider to transfer a copy of all of my medical records with me in such instance. I specifically indemnify and hold harmless any medical care facility releasing me for such purpose.

11. *Careful Consideration Has Been Made of Decisions in This Document.*
These decisions and requests are made after careful consideration and reflection. These decisions are made to avoid the indignity, pain, and difficulties, both for myself and my family, of prolonged, hopeless deterioration and dependence where I am in a condition described above.

12. *Religious Convictions.*

[Select a provision that best reflects your wishes and delete the remaining provisions. Revise as necessary.]

a.   *No Religious Restrictions Should Apply.*
I do not wish to condition the effectiveness of this directive upon its conforming to any _____ [religion your agents or family believe you are associated with] or other religious doctrines or beliefs to which I may be believed to subscribe.

b.   *Religious Principles Shall Apply to the Interpretation of This Living Will.*
I wish to condition the effectiveness of this directive upon its conforming to [religion your agents or family believe you are associated with] doctrines and beliefs to which I subscribe. In order to effectuate my wishes, if any question arises as to the requirements of my religious beliefs, I direct that my health care Agent consult with and follow the guidance of:
[ ] a religious adviser selected in my Agent's reasonable discretion and in accordance with my statement of religious beliefs made in this paragraph
[ ] the following person, _____ [religious adviser's name]
[ ] If such person is unable, unwilling, or unavailable to provide such consultation and guidance, then I direct my Agent to consult with and follow the guidance of the person appointed by the following religious institution: _____ [institution's name].

I expressly state that no health care provider shall be required in any situation to require any approval from such religious adviser in order to carry out the instructions of any Agent hereunder.

13. *Organ Donations.*

[Select a provision that best reflects your wishes and delete the remaining provisions. Revise as necessary.]

a.   To carry out my wish to be an organ and tissue donor upon my death by informing the attending medical personnel that I am a donor. To execute such papers and do such acts as shall be necessary, appropriate, incidental, or convenient in connection with such gifts. To make anatomical gifts that will take effect at my death for the sole purpose of:
[ ] transplant to save another person's life
[ ] medical study or education

[ ] any needed organs and tissues
[ ] only the following organs and tissues: _____ [list organs and tissues to be donated].

14. *Funeral, Cremation, and Related Arrangements.*

[Select a provision that best reflects your wishes and delete the remaining provisions. Revise as necessary.]

[ ] *No Religious Principles Shall Apply to Funeral and Other Arrangements.*
[ ] Notwithstanding any statements above concerning inapplicability of religious doctrines, I specifically request that my funeral service and arrangements and burial be in accordance with _____ [name of religion] religious customs.
[ ] My funeral service should be in accordance with _____ [name of religion] religious customs.
[ ] My Agent is hereby authorized to purchase a burial plot and marker, and to make such other related arrangements as my Agent shall deem appropriate, if I have not already done so myself.
[ ] I recognize that any ceremony is for the benefit of those surviving in that ritualized or communal mourning may help them to pass through their personal grief to a state of acceptance. Accordingly, I defer in all respects to the wishes of my survivors in this regard, and I ask that they make whatever arrangements will give them the greatest solace.
[ ] Cremation and interment of my remains, including the purchase of a place of interment.

15. *No Time Limit; Duration.*
I have considered the possibility of limiting the effectiveness of this instrument to a fixed period of time from the date hereof and have decided that it shall remain in full force and effect for as long as I may live and may be so relied upon by any person or institution unless such person or institution has actually received a written notice of revocation or change.

16. *Morally Binding.*
These directions are the exercise of my right to refuse treatment. Therefore, I expect my family, physicians, and all those concerned with my care to regard themselves as legally (whether or not required by the law at the time of the execution, or the place of implementation, of this Living Will) and morally bound to act in accordance with these directions, and in so doing to be free from any liability and responsibility for having followed my Wishes.

17. *Revocation of Prior Grants.*
This document revokes any prior living will, health care power of attorney, or health care proxy executed by me.

18. *Copies of Document.*
A copy of this document shall be as valid as the original. I ask that a copy of this document be made part of my permanent medical record.

19. *Severability.*

The provisions of this entire document are separable so that the invalidity of one or more provisions shall not affect any others.

20. *Competency to Execute Document.*

I understand the full import of this document, and I am emotionally and mentally competent to execute it.

21. *Construction and Interpretation of this Document.*

a.   Should legislation or regulations be enacted after the execution of this Living Will, then this Living Will shall, to the extent necessary to make it valid and enforceable, be interpreted so as to comply with such future legislation or regulations in the manner that most closely approximates my Wishes.

b.   The titles and captions contained in this article are for convenience only and should not be read to affect the meaning of any provision.

c.   Should any provision in this Living Will be declared invalid or unenforceable, the remaining provisions shall not be affected so long as they can be applied in a manner to carry out my Wishes as set forth herein.

d.   This Living Will is executed in _____ [state name] and should be interpreted in accordance with the laws of such state, unless my agent designates the laws of a different state to apply.

IN WITNESS WHEREOF, I have executed this declaration _____ [month] _____ [day], _____ [year].

_____ [your signature]

Witness: _____

State of   )
             :
County of   )

On this _____ [month] _____ [day], _____ [year], before me, the subscriber, a notary of the State of _____ [state name], personally appeared [your name], who, I am satisfied is the principal mentioned in, and who signed the Living Will and acknowledged that he or she signed, sealed, and delivered the same as his or her act and deed, that he or she appeared to be of sound mind and not under any duress, fraud, or undue influence, and for the uses and purposes therein expressed.

_____

Notary Signature

DECLARATION OF WITNESSES TO LIVING
WILL FOR MEDICAL DECISIONS

The undersigned each hereby declare and attest that: (1) the Living Will was personally signed, sealed, and delivered by _____ [your name], in my presence, and, at _____ [your name]'s request and in _____ [your name]'s presence and in the presence of the other witnesses, I subscribed my name as a witness; (2) I did not sign the signature of _____ [your name]; (3) I am acquainted with _____ [your name] and believe _____ [your name] to be of sound mind and under no constraint, duress, or undue influence; (4) I am not related to _____ [your name] by blood or marriage; (5) I am not, to the best of my knowledge, entitled to any portion of the estate of _____ [your name] under any Will of _____ [your name] or Codicil now existing, nor am I so entitled by operation of law; (6) I do not have any present or inchoate claim against any portion of _____ [your name]'s estate or for _____ [your name]'s medical care; (7) I am not a physician attending to _____ [your name] as a patient; and (8) I am over eighteen (18) years of age.

Printed Name of Witness	Address (City and State) of Witness	Signature of Witness

TEAR-OUT ORGAN DONOR CARD

LIVING WILL/HEALTH CARE PROXY INFORMATION:

[ ] I have executed a Living Will

[ ] I have executed a Health Care Proxy and appointed:

_____
Name of Agent

(day) _____   (night) _____
Telephone Numbers for Agent

_____
Name of Alternate Agent

(day) _____   (night) _____
Telephone Numbers for Alternate Agent

My Agent has a copy of my Health Care Proxy
[ ] Yes   [ ] No

My Alternate Agent has a copy of my Health Care Proxy
[ ] Yes   [ ] No

_____   _____
Date   My Printed Name

_____
Signature

My [ ] Living Will and/or [ ] Health Care Proxy
can be found:

_____
Location of Living Will and/or Health Care Proxy

Other copies can be found with:

_____
(Name)   (Telephone No.)

_____
(Name)   (Telephone No.)

TEAR-OUT ORGAN DONOR CARD

Side One	Side Two
This is a legal document under the Uniform Anatomical Gift Act signed by the donor and the following two witnesses in the presence of each other:	Please type or print full name of donor.
	In the hope that I may help others, I hereby make this gift for the purpose of transplant, medical study, or education, to take effect upon my death.
	I give: [ ] Any needed organs/tissues [ ] only the following organs/tissues
	_____
	Specify the organ(s)/tissues:
_____ Donor's signature	Limitations or special wishes, if any:
_____ Donor's date of birth	
_____ City and state	
_____ Witness	
_____ Witness	
_____ Next of Kin	

TEAR-OUT HEALTH CARE PROXY

Health Care Proxy—Durable Power of Attorney for Medical Decisions.

I, _____ [your name] residing at _____ [your address], to provide for management of my person, body, health, and medical affairs in a more orderly fashion, hereby declare as follows:

    1. *Appointment of Attorney-in-Fact and Agent.*

I hereby make, constitute, and appoint ("Grant") _____ [name of first agent], residing at _____ [address of first agent], as my true and lawful Attorney-in-Fact and Health Care Agent for me and in my name, place, and stead and for my benefit, or any alternate appointed in accordance with the provisions of this agreement (the "Agent").

Telephone Numbers:

Work/Day:

Evening/Home:

Cell:

Pager:

---

    2. *Appointment of Alternate Attorney-in-Fact and Health Care Agent.*

      a. If _____ [name of first agent] is unwilling or unable to act as my Agent, I appoint the first person on the following list who is able and willing to serve as my Alternate Agent:

          (1) _____ [name of second agent], who resides at _____ [address of second agent].

Telephone Numbers:

Work/Day:

Evening/Home:

Cell:

Pager:

---

(2) _____ [name of third agent], who resides at _____ [address of third agent].

> Telephone Numbers:
>
> Work/Day:
>
> Evening/Home:
>
> Cell:
>
> Pager:

I request, but do not require, that any Agent appointed above endeavor to consult with _____ [person to consult with], where feasible, prior to taking any action.

b.   Any reference to Agent shall include the Alternate Agent where such Alternate Agent is acting as provided under this durable power of attorney for medical decisions.

c.   If all of the above Agents have predeceased me or are unable or unwilling for any reason to serve as my Agent, but an agent is required by law solely in order to direct the withholding or withdrawal of life-sustaining treatment, or other medical or health care objectives, in accordance with my Wishes, I authorize my attending physician to appoint such an Agent upon consultation with one or more of my relatives, religious advisers (if any are specified herein), friends, or other persons or agencies reasonably believed to be interested in my well-being.

3.   *Powers of Agent.*

[Modify or delete as appropriate to be certain that the powers granted to your agent are consistent with your wishes.]

a.   I grant to my Agent all the powers and rights necessary to effect my wishes.

b.   I grant to my Agent full power and authority to do, take, and perform each and every act and thing whatsoever requisite, proper, or necessary to be done, in the exercise of any of the rights and powers herein granted, necessary to carry out my Wishes, and available under law to an agent, acting in such capacity and for the purposes herein indicated. I grant my Agent the authority to act as fully, and for all reasons and purposes as I might or could act if I were personally present and able, to the extent not inconsistent with my preferences, including the powers to do, by way of example and not limitation, the following: _____ [detail of any special wishes, religious preferences, etc.].

(1)   To authorize a "Do not resuscitate" or "No code" order.

(2)   To give or withhold consent to any medical procedure test or treatment, including surgery, to the extent permitted in accordance with my preferences, in accordance with my request to have all medically appropriate heroic measures given. To arrange for my hospitalization, convalescent care, hospice care, or home care. To summon paramedics or other emergency medical personnel and seek emergency treatment for me, or to restrict such emergency treatment by paramedics or other emergency medical personnel in accordance with my Wishes.

(3)   To withdraw, modify, or change consent to any medical procedure, test and treatment, hospitalization, convalescent care, hospice, home care, or other treatment that either I or my Agent may have arranged.

(4)   To grant, change, or withdraw informed consent to any procedure or treatment.

(5)   To make all necessary arrangements for me at any hospital, hospice, nursing home (including veterans nursing care facility, or any state- or federally run facility), convalescent home, or similar establishment, including my transfer and removal, and to ensure that all my essential needs are provided for at such a facility.

(6)   To provide for companionship that will meet my needs and preferences at such time when I am disabled or otherwise unable to arrange for such companionship myself.

(7)   To employ and discharge medical personnel, including physicians, psychiatrists, dentists, nurses, and therapists as my Agent shall deem necessary for my physical, mental, and emotional well-being.

(8)   To make advance arrangement for treatment of my remains as provided for in my Living Will.

(9)   To inquire as to whether the cemetery or cemeteries where my family are buried or interred are fulfilling their responsibilities under any applicable perpetual care contracts in existence, to take any actions to ensure same, and to direct the Fiduciary under my Last Will and Testament to make any reasonable payments toward same.

(10) To carry out my wish to be an organ and tissue donor upon my death by informing the attending medical personnel that I am a donor. To execute such papers and do such acts as shall be necessary, appropriate, incidental, or convenient in connection with such gifts. To make anatomical gifts.

(11) To order whatever is appropriate to keep me as comfortable and free of pain as is reasonably possible, including the administration of pain-relieving drugs, surgical or medical procedures calculated to relieve my pain, and unconventional pain-relief therapies that my Agent believes may be helpful.

(12) My Agent shall be entitled to sign, execute, deliver, and acknowledge any contract or other document that may be necessary, desirable, convenient, or proper in order to exercise any of the powers described in this Health Care Proxy and to incur reasonable costs in the exercise of any such powers.

(13) To request, receive, and review any information regarding my medical, physical, or mental health, including but not limited to hospital records, and to execute any release or other documents that may be required in order to

obtain such information and to disclose such information to such persons, organizations, and others as my Agent shall deem appropriate.

4. *Guardian and Conservator.*

To the extent that I am permitted by law to do so, I hereby nominate my Agent to serve as my guardian, special medical guardian, conservator, or in any similar representative capacity, and if I am not permitted by law to so nominate, then I request that any court that may be involved in the appointment of a guardian, special medical guardian, conservator, or similar representative for me give the greatest weight to this request. Where my Agent is unable or unwilling to so serve, I hereby nominate my Alternate Agent to so serve. Any such person appointed shall serve without bond. It is my express intent that the appointment of a guardian or conservator not serve to revoke or supersede any separate durable Power of Attorney for financial matters if I have in fact executed such document and such document remains in force. Rather, it is my intent that such separate durable Power of Attorney for financial matters continue to govern for the matters addressed herein, and the appointment of a conservator or guardian be solely for the purposes of governing personal, medical, and other such matters.

5. *Approval.*

I hereby ratify and confirm all that said Attorney-in-Fact shall lawfully do or cause to be done by virtue of this Health Care Proxy and the rights and powers herein granted.

6. *Grant of Medical Decisions Powers.*

I specifically designate my Agent to make medical treatment decisions for me in the event that I am comatose or otherwise unable to make such decisions for myself, including any decisions with respect to life-sustaining measures, artificial feeding, artificial hydration, and other matters.

7. *Indemnification of Agent.*

I hereby agree to indemnify and hold harmless the Agent (including any Alternate Agent acting hereunder) for any actions taken, or not taken, where such Agent acted in good faith and was not guilty of fraud, gross negligence, or willful misconduct.

8. *Construction and Interpretation of This Document.*

This instrument is to be construed and interpreted as a durable general Power of Attorney for medical, health care, and related matters. The enumeration of specific items, rights, acts, or powers herein is not intended to, nor does it limit or restrict, and is not to be construed or interpreted as limiting or restricting the general powers herein granted to said Agent. This instrument is executed and delivered in the State of _____ [name of state], and the laws of such state shall govern all questions as to the validity of this power and the construction of its provisions, unless changed by my agent. Should any provision or power in this document not be enforceable, such enforceability shall not affect the enforceability of the rest of this document. In this regard, I specifically state that I have granted my Agent certain authority and power over my health and personal matters to ensure the carrying out of my Wishes. Should this grant be prohibited by any law presently existing or hereinafter enacted, it is my specific desire that such grant be interpreted in the broadest manner permitted by such law, and that in the event such grant is prohibited, that every other provision of this Health Care Proxy remain fully valid and enforceable.

9. *Other People Relying on This Document.*

Third parties, including but not limited to medical professionals, hospitals, convalescent facilities, nursing homes, hospices, or the like, may rely on the representations of my Agent as to all matters relating to any power granted to my Agent as my Agent, Attorney-in-Fact, and Health Care Agent, and no person who may act in reliance upon the representations of my Agent or the authority granted to my Agent shall incur any liability to me or my estate as a result of permitting my Agent to exercise any power conveyed under this Health Care Proxy.

10. *Inspection and Photocopies of Documents and Records.*

a.   My Agent shall have the authority to request and inspect any reports, files, or other records regarding my condition and is hereby authorized to execute any documents, releases, or other approvals or prerequisites to such inspections.

b.   My Agent is authorized to make photocopies of this Health Care Proxy as such Agent deems necessary and appropriate to carrying out my Wishes. Any third party may rely on a duly executed counterpart of this instrument, and a copy thereof where such copy is certified by my Agent, as being a true copy of the original hereof, as fully and completely as if such third party had received the original of this instrument.

11. *Disability Does Not Affect Validity of This Document.*

This Power of Attorney shall not, to the extent permitted by applicable law, be affected by my disability as principal, and I do hereby so provide, it being my intention that all powers conferred upon my Agent herein or any substitute designated by me shall remain at all times in full force and effect, notwithstanding my incapacity, disability, or any uncertainty with regard thereto. This provision shall be interpreted in the broadest terms so as to remain in effect throughout my disability to the fullest extent provided for under the laws of the state.

12. *Resignation of Agent.*

Any Agent may resign by providing written notice to me (or my guardian or committee) with copy to the next named Agent or a court of competent jurisdiction.

13. *No Compensation.*

No Agent shall receive any compensation for the performance of the acts, rights, or responsibilities set forth herein, but any Agent may be reimbursed for actual and necessary expenses incurred in the performance of such Agent's acts, rights, and responsibilities.

14. *Cooperation of Health Care Agent and Financial Agent.*

If I have executed a separate financial Power of Attorney form or document appointing any person or entity to serve as my financial agent or attorney-in-fact, I request that my Agent appointed herein cooperate with such financial agent and keep such financial agent reasonably advised of expenses incurred, or likely to be incurred, in connection with my health care and related matters by my Agent under the powers granted in this Health Care Proxy.

15. *Effective Date of This Document.*
This Health Care Proxy shall be effective as of the date it is executed.

16. *Revocation of Prior Grants.*
This document revokes any prior living will, health care power of attorney, or health care proxy executed by me.

17. *Copies of Document.*
A copy of this document shall be as valid as the original. I ask that a copy of this document be made part of my permanent medical record.

18. *Severability.*
The provisions of this entire document are separable so that the invalidity of one or more provisions shall not affect any others.

19. *Competency to Execute Document.*
I understand the full import of this document, and I am emotionally and mentally competent to execute it.

20. *Termination of Grant to Agent.*
a.   As to any health care Agent (or any successor Agent), this Health Care Proxy shall be modified or terminated, as the case may be, upon my executing a document terminating the Grant or upon my executing a written notice of modification or revocation and such Agent's receipt of same.
b.   As to any health care provider, this Health Care Proxy shall be modified or terminated, as the case may be, upon such health care provider actually receiving notice of a modification or termination.
c.   If my spouse has been designated as an Agent or Alternate Agent hereunder, if subsequent to the execution of this document, my spouse and I are legally separated or divorced, any rights and powers granted to my spouse shall immediately terminate on such legal separation or divorce.
d.   I have considered the possibility of limiting the effectiveness of this instrument to a fixed period of time from the date hereof and have decided that it shall remain in full force and effect for as long as I may live unless terminated as provided above.
IN WITNESS WHEREOF, I have hereunto set my hand and seal this _____ [month] _____ [day], _____ [year].

_____ [your name]

Witness: _____

State of   )
                    :
County of   )

BE IT REMEMBERED, that on this _____ [month] _____ [day], _____ [year], before me, the subscriber, a notary of the State of _____ [name of state], personally appeared _____ [your name], who, I am satisfied is the principal mentioned in, and who executed the above Health Care Proxy and acknowledged that he or she signed, sealed, and delivered the same as his or her act and deed, that he or she appeared to be of sound mind and not under any duress, fraud, or undue influence, and for the uses and purposes therein expressed.

_____
Notary Signature

21. *Declaration of Witnesses to Health Care Proxy Durable Power of Attorney for Medical Decisions.*

The undersigned each hereby declare and attest that: (1) the Health Care Proxy was personally signed, sealed, and delivered by _____ [your name], in my presence, and, at such person's request, and in such person's presence and in the presence of the other witnesses, I subscribed my name as a witness; (2) I did not sign the signature of such person; (3) I am acquainted with such person and believe such person to be of sound mind and under no constraint, duress, or undue influence; (4) I am not related to such person by blood or marriage; (5) I am not, to the best of my knowledge, entitled to any portion of the estate of such person under any Will of such person or Codicil now existing, nor am I so entitled by operation of law; (6) I do not have any present or inchoate claim against any portion of such person's estate or for such person's medical care; (7) I am not a physician attending to such person as a patient; and (8) I am over eighteen (18) years of age.

Printed Name of Witness	Address (City and State) of Witness	Signature of Witness

TEAR-OUT CHILD MEDICAL FORM

AUTHORIZATION FOR EMERGENCY CARE OF MINOR CHILD

A.　*Authorization by Parent To Care For Children.*

I _____ [your name] and _____ [other parent's name] (collectively and individually "Parent"), residing at _____ [your address], make and declare this my medical authorization, directive, and instruction (my "Authorization") concerning the care of _____ [children's names] (individually and collectively "Child").

B.　*Agent to Authorize Medical Care for Children.*

If I am not available in the event of a medical need, I authorize and direct that any doctor, hospital, emergency room facility, ambulance, or other medical care provider ("Medical Care Provider") rely on the instructions of the first person in the following list who is able and willing and available to act ("Agent") in caring for any Child in a medical emergency or until I can reasonably be contacted. If any person on the list below is not available, the medical care provider should contact the next person. The term *available* shall be determined in the reasonable discretion of the medical care provider.

Name	Relationship	Home Address	Telephone Numbers
			Work: Home: Vacation: Cellular:
			Work: Home: Vacation: Cellular:
			Work: Home: Vacation: Cellular:
			Work: Home: Vacation: Cellular:

C.   *Insurance Coverage.*

Insurance Carrier Name
Name of Insured
Policy Number

D.   *Powers and Rights of Agents.*
1.   To make all necessary arrangements for the Child at any hospital, emergency room, or other health care facility, or similar establishment, including the transfer and removal of any Child from one such facility to another, and any decision reasonably necessary to ensure that all the Child's essential needs are provided for at such a facility.
2.   To give or withhold consent to any medical procedures test or treatment, including surgery. To arrange for the hospitalizations and medical and related care, of the Child. To summon paramedics or other emergency medical personnel and seek emergency treatment for the Child. To withdraw, modify, or change consent to any medical procedure, test and treatment, hospitalization, convalescent care, home care, or other treatment which I, the Child, or another person may have arranged for the Child.
3.   My Agent shall be entitled to sign, execute, deliver, and acknowledge any contract or other document that may be necessary, desirable, convenient, or proper in order to exercise any of the powers described in this Authorization and to incur reasonable costs in the carrying out of this Authorization.
4.   The Agent, however, shall not be permitted to take the following actions or make the following decisions ("Exclusions") [If none listed, no exclusions shall apply]:

E.   *No Time Limit.*
I have considered the possibility of limiting the effectiveness of this instrument to a fixed period of time from the date hereof and have decided that it shall remain in full force and effect until revoked.

F. *Authorization and Direction Binding.*

I expect my family, physicians, and all those concerned with the care of my Child to regard themselves as legally (whether or not required by the law at the time of the execution, or the place of implementation, of this Authorization) and morally bound to act in accordance with these directions, and in so doing to be free from any liability and responsibility for having followed my wishes stated herein.

G. *Third Parties.*

Third parties, including but not limited to medical professionals, insurance companies, hospitals, convalescent facilities, or the like, may rely upon the representations of an Agent as to all matters relating to any power granted to an Agent acting in the capacity as the Agent for my Child.

H. *Construction.*

This Agreement shall be governed under the laws of the State of _____ [state name]. This Agreement may be executed in one or more counterparts. Should any provision contained in this Authorization be unenforceable, such unenforceability shall not affect the enforceability of the remainder of this Authorization. The use of *male, female,* singular, or plural shall be interpreted as the usage requires.

I. *Acknowledgment of Parents and Affidavits of Witnesses.*

I, being first duly sworn, do hereby declare that I am the parent and legal guardian of the Child named in this Authorization, that I have executed this Authorization instrument willingly, as my free and voluntary act for the purposes herein expressed, that at the time of said execution I am eighteen (18) years of age or older, of sound mind, and under no constraint or undue influence.

_____ [your signature]

_____ [other parent's signature]

State of   )
                :ss.:
County of   )

On this _____ [month] _____ [day], _____ [year], before me personally came, _____ [your name] and _____ [other parent's name], the Parent, to me known and known to me to be the individual described in and who executed the foregoing Authorization in my presence. The Parent duly acknowledged, subscribed, and swore before me that he or she understood the meaning of the Authorization and executed the same before me.

_____
Notary Public

MEDICAL HISTORY AND RELATED INFORMATION

Child Name			
Blood Type			
Allergies			
Existing Medical Conditions			
Medications Taken			
Child's Past Medical History			
Smoke/Drinking/Drug Use			
Family Medical History			
Religious Restrictions on Care			
Child's Social History			
Other Comments			
Tips on How to Comfort Child (favorite toys, etc.)			

GLOSSARY

Advance directives: A document in which you communicate your health care wishes in a clear and convincing manner that, if later you are not competent to make those decisions, will enable you to exercise your right to self-determination.

Affidavit: A sworn statement in the presence of a notary public or someone authorized to officiate sworn statements.

Anatomical gifts: Gifts having to do with the human body. Usually refers to organ donation.

Beneficiary: A person who receives the benefits of a trust or of transfers under your will.

Benefits and burdens: When assessing whether a particular medical treatment should be continued, the benefits the treatment may provide may be weighed against the burdens the continuation of the treatment may create. This type of test can lead to the determination that certain medical treatments, even if not entirely futile, might best be avoided. This benefits and burdens analysis can be applied to the specific facts of a particular patient, without the use of some of the commonly used, but vague and confusing terms, such as *no heroic measures*. If a particular treatment is not considered *heroic* (i.e., instead, it is *ordinary*), it would have to be given. In contrast, if a benefits and burdens test were instead used, the same treatment, whether ordinary or heroic, could be given or refused depending on the impact on the patient. On the other hand, the benefits and burdens test may not provide much insight for a young trauma victim in a persistent vegetative state. The only benefit is mere physical life itself, and individuals differ as to whether that is a benefit. Thus, what

215

might be a benefit to a clergyman might be viewed as a burden to a family member and perhaps even differently by a physician.

Best interests: If there is no clear and convincing evidence of a patient's health care wishes, a surrogate decision maker can make a decision only on the basis of what is preferable for the patient or what is in the patient's best interests.

Brain death: The irreversible loss of all brain function or activity. Oxygen supply to the brain is cut off and electrical activity is nonexistent. The body is nonfunctional as a result. Brain death is accepted as the legal definition of death in most states.

Capacity: The mental or physical ability to understand or perform certain actions. In the context of advance directives, having sufficient capacity enables you to exercise informed consent to your medical care.

Cardiopulmonary resuscitation (CPR): Reviving a failed heart by breathing into the lungs of the victim and applying chest compressions, which circulates blood and oxygen to the body.

Case law: Laws established by the rulings of different courts in contrast to laws enacted by a state or federal legislature.

Clear and convincing evidence: If a patient made statements as to his or her desire for particular medical treatment while competent, there is evidence of what those wishes were, the evidence is specific enough, the statements were not too casual and were reasonably to be applied to the patient's conditions, those statements may provide sufficient clear and convincing proof of the patient's wishes.

Code: Medical jargon used to indicate that a patient's heart has stopped pumping or the patient has stopped breathing, and CPR or other life-saving procedures must be applied to try to revive it.

Committee: Court-appointed person(s) to manage the affairs of another, usually due to the lack of capacity of that person.

Competency: The mental capacity to comprehend the nature and ramifications of your actions.

Conflict of interest: A compromising motive. For example, courts generally view family members as the most appropriate surrogates to make medical decisions for an incompetent patient. However, family members, especially those standing to inherit assets of the patient's estate, have serious conflicts of interest.

Conservator: See *guardian* or *committee.*

Constitution: Federal or state constitution that establishes fundamental rights of citizens. These fundamental rights, for example, the right to privacy provided in some constitutions or read into the United States Constitution through case law, are the basis for many key end-of-life rights.

Defibrillation: Shocking the heart electronically to reestablish normal heart rhythm.

Dementia: The loss of brain functions, for example, memory, decision-making, verbal communication, and judgment. Usually caused by disease or trauma.

Domicile: The principal place of abode. May be defined as a stronger connection than merely residing.

Donor: A person who makes a gift, such as donating an organ.

Do not resuscitate (DNR): A directive ordering that life support measures such as cardiopulmonary resuscitation (CPR) not be instituted after a cardiac (heart) or respiratory (lung) arrest.

Durable power of attorney: A document in which you grant certain people the authority to handle your financial matters. If a power of attorney is durable, it remains valid even if you become disabled. Should not be combined with a living will or health care proxy.

Durable power of attorney for medical decisions: A document in which you grant certain people the authority to handle your medical and health care decisions, also called a *health care proxy.* Should not be confused with, in spite of the similar name, a power of attorney for financial matters.

Electroencephalogram: A test that measures the electrical activity of the brain.

Euthanasia: Taking another person's life to spare him or her incurable and insufferable pain. Considered a crime and clearly violates a physician's professional ethics.

Executor or executrix (feminine): A person designated to manage your estate upon your death (marshalling assets, paying expenses and taxes, and making distributions to beneficiaries). Sometimes called *administrator* or *personal administrator.*

Fiduciary: A person in a position of trust and responsibility, such as the executor of your will, the trustee of a trust, or the agent under a living will.

Futile treatment: Medical care that cannot and does not improve the prognosis for recovery. Medical ethics may not mandate that a physician continue futile treatment.

Gift: A benefit or anything of value given to another without the expectation of receiving compensation in return.

Give: To transfer ownership to another.

Guardian: The person you designate as responsible for your minor children or other person requiring special care. Also used in connection with a person appointed as a guardian for assets.

Guardian ad litem: Latin phrase for "guardian of the suit," usually referring to someone appointed to prosecute or defend a suit on behalf of a person who is incapable. In our context, it refers to a court-appointed guardian for a specific purpose.

Guardianship: The process of having a court appoint a person to be responsible for a disabled person or minor. See *conservator* or *committee.*

Health care proxy: A written instrument giving authorization to a specified individual to act and make decisions on your behalf.

Heirs: The persons who receive your assets following your death. An heir should not be witness to your living will or health care proxy.

Heroic measures: Advanced cardiac or respiratory measures, such as intubation, ventilation, medications, and other steps, when there is little hope for survival. Be careful, as the definitions can be vague and may differ depending on the person making the interpretation.

Hospice care: A facility or program that delivers palliative care, such as pain relief and counseling, for patients with end-stage disease or terminal conditions. Can include personal support for the patient and the family. May include bereavement support.

Hydration: Administering fluids to the patient by way of and not limited to feeding tubes, Corpak tubes, nasogastric tubes, Levin tubes, gastrostomy tubes, or hyperalimentation. Many health care providers consider hydration mere nursing care, and not medical care, such that it should be provided to all patients.

Hyperalimentation: Providing electrolytes, vitamins, and nutrients, in liquid form, through the veins.

Impairment: The diminishing of a particular sense (seeing or hearing), trait, or function.

Inchoate: In an early stage. Beginning to exist.

Incompetent: Not having the mental capacity to comprehend the nature and ramifications of your actions. An incompetent patient does not have the ability to exercise his or her right of self-determination. Some courts have permitted a substitute or surrogate person to exercise this right on behalf of the incompetent patient.

Indemnify: To protect against an anticipated loss or to reimburse for an actual loss.

Informed consent: A patient's knowledgeable agreement to a particular medical care.

Intubation: A procedure that makes use of a tube to breathe for a person.

Irrevocable: Where a legal document cannot be changed after you've signed or established it.

Life-sustaining treatment: The use of any procedures (e.g., CPR, hydration, nutrition), medical devices, or surgery that artificially sustains important bodily functions to increase a patient's life span.

Living will: A document in which you can specify life-saving measures you do, and do not, wish to be taken on your behalf in the event of extreme illness. Compare *health care proxy* (or power of attorney).

Lucidity: Clarity of the mind. Having sound judgment.

Majority: The age of being an adult—18 in many states.

Medical power of attorney: Another term used for a health care power of attorney or health care proxy.

Minor: Person who is not old enough to be an adult under state law. Age varies by state. Without legal authority, a minor cannot make advance directives or give informed consent. The parent may have to take these actions on behalf of the minor.

Next of kin: A legal term describing the person who is in closest relation to the deceased.

Notary: Public officer or clerk who attests or certifies a document.

Nutrition: Administering foods to the patient by way of and not limited to feeding tubes, Corpak tubes, nasogastric tubes, Levin tubes, gastrostomy tubes, or hyperalimentation (see previous definition). Many health care providers consider nutrition to be mere nursing care, and not medical care, so that it should be provided to all patients.

Palliative care: Trying to relieve the pain and symptoms of a medical condition or a disease without curing it. A holistic approach of taking care of the entire person, not just the physical aspects of the person. Includes taking care of the spirit, mind, and heart, not just the body. Palliative care views dying as a natural event, not something to avoid talking about.

Patient advocate: A person who agrees (usually by way of a formal agreement) to implement the medical wishes of the patient; an agent.

Per stirpes: A term of inheritance. The child receives the share that his or her parent would have inherited had the parent survived the decedent. X intends to leave 10 percent of his estate to Y. Y dies before X, so Y's child, Z, inherits the 10 percent *per stirpes.*

Principal: The person who signs a health care proxy and appoints an agent to make decisions for him or her.

Probate: The judicial process of having a will legally certified.

Proxy: A person named to serve as your agent to make health care decisions if you are unable to.

Quality of life: A personal decision as to the level of participation in life functions.

Renunciation: To decline a legal obligation or benefit.

Severability: The ability of a contract to be subdivided into multiple parts so that the invalidity of one part does not affect the validity of any other part.

Springing power of attorney: A document in which you grant certain people the authority to handle your financial matters, which becomes effective only if you are disabled.

Substituted judgment: An approach used in some court cases to address end-of-life decision making when the patient cannot, and will never be able to, make decisions. The court may vest in the parents the rights to make a decision on behalf of such a patient, hence, a *substituted decision* for the patient.

Surrogate decision maker: When a patient is incompetent to make his or her own medical care decisions, the courts may appoint a substitute or surrogate to make decisions on behalf of the patient.

Terminal illness: An irreversible, incurable, and untreatable condition caused by disease, illness, or injury from which there is no hope of recovery, or death is likely to occur in a brief period of time if life-sustaining treatment is not provided.

Unconscious: A state such that you are unaware of yourself and your environment.

Vegetative state: No cerebral cortical function (no higher order brain function).

Withdrawing treatment: Intentionally ceasing or withdrawing medical or life support treatment, such as a feeding tube or a respirator.

Withholding treatment: Intentionally refusing to give medical or other life-sustaining treatment.

Witness: One who observes, usually by sight or sound, a particular event and signs his or her name to a document that describes the event, thereby affirming the veracity of it.

INDEX